God & America

By Paul E Chapman

AddtoYourFaith.com

© 2020

God & America

Paul E Chapman

Published by:
Add To Your Faith Publications
P.O. Box 5369
S. Kingstown, RI, USA

AddToYourFaith.com

Typesetting: Add To Your Faith

Cover Design: PaulEChapman.com

Printed in USA

Dedicated To

*The God of Heaven Who Birthed Our Nation
& His Son Jesus Christ Who Died To Save Our
Souls. Also, To The Countless Americans Who
Served In The U.S. Armed Forces And God's Army
Hazarding Life And Limb To Protect Our Country.*

Contents

CHAPTER I

God & America

2 Chronicles 7:14

If my people, which are called by my name, shall humble themselves, and pray, and seek my face, and turn from their wicked ways; then will I hear from heaven, and will forgive their sin, and will heal their land.

God and America are uniquely linked. Some attempt to change history to deny this extraordinary relationship. If America hopes to survive, she must turn back to the God Who gave her life.

America is a great nation. In every measurable statistic, our nation has been uniquely blessed. America is great because of its great God. We wouldn't even exist as a country if it were not for the miraculous work of the Lord.

After years of religious apathy, moral decay, and ungodly attack, America is fighting for her life. Will she remain a Christian nation, or reject her God?

God's plan of salvation for individuals is simple faith in the death, burial, and resurrection of Jesus Christ for the remission of sins.

Our text explains God's plan of salvation for a nation. God speaks much about nations in the Scripture. They can be blessed or cursed.

1

They can be built or destroyed. The only hope for America is a religious revival, according to 2 Chronicles 7:14.

Before we look at our text verse, let's view our nation through the light of God's Word. Consider these facts.

1. GOD CHOSE THE COUNTRY ISRAEL TO REPRESENT HIM IN THE OLD TESTAMENT.

Psalm 135:4

For the Lord hath chosen Jacob unto himself, And Israel for his peculiar treasure.

Deuteronomy 10:15

Only the Lord had a delight in thy fathers to love them, and he chose their seed after them, even you above all people, as it is this day.

God chose the nation of Israel to represent Him in the Old Testament. God made an everlasting covenant with them.

God spoke through Israel to the other nations of the world. He gave them the oracles of God. The Messiah came through Israel also. Never has there been a nation so blessed!

2. IN THE NEW TESTAMENT, EVERY CHRISTIAN IS GOD'S AMBASSADOR.

2 Corinthians 5:19–20

To wit, that God was in Christ, reconciling the world unto himself, not imputing their trespasses unto them; and hath committed unto us the word of reconciliation. Now then we are ambassadors for Christ, as though God did beseech you by us: we pray you in Christ's stead, be ye reconciled to God.

In the New Testament age, Christians are the representatives of God. We are His ambassadors.

An ambassador is an official representative of a monarch or nation representing the power and relaying the sovereign's messages while living in a foreign country.

That's who we are! We represent the Lord of glory in this sinful world.

3. God has uniquely blessed America and used her to spread the Gospel around the world.

God was involved in America from the beginning. Consider the following facts about our blessed country.

Miraculous Conception.

Pericles led a civilization built upon culture and it fell. Alexander the Great built a empire by military genius and it perished. Ceasar built a kingdom built upon power and it died. Yet, there was something different about birth of America. It was built by men who fled from tyranny to serve God according to His Word and their consciences.

Fifty-six men hazarded their lives by signing the Declaration of Independence. Most sacrificed everything to stand for this idea of a free America.

Benjamin Franklin was 81 years old at the Constitutional Convention of 1787 in Philadelphia. He urged the assembly to pray daily and seek guidance from "the Father."

He famously said, *"I have lived a long time, Sir, a long time, and the longer I live, the more convincing proofs I see of this truth—that God governs in the affairs of men. And if a sparrow cannot fall to the ground without His notice, is it probable that an empire can rise without his aid?"*

An act of God birthed America. It is a miracle she exists.

Divine Protection.

God has protected America supernaturally.

In the Revolutionary War, God allowed us to defeat the most powerful country on Earth to become a sovereign nation.

In World War 1 and World War 2, God allowed us to beat superior forces.

America became a superpower without equal in the world due to the providence of God.

Supernatural Production.

America has developed supernaturally. Investigate how the U.S. grew to the land it now holds. It is incredible.

Think of all the great inventions that have come from America. We have changed the world with creativity, insight, and technology.

The American economy is the envy of the world.

Did all this happen without the aid of the Almighty? I think not.

Godly Intention.

Christian men founded America on the principles of the King James Bible. Don't fall for the lies of those who attempt to revise history.

Proverbs 14:34

Righteousness exalteth a nation: but sin is a reproach to any people.

Alexis de Tocqueville was a 19th-century French diplomat. He is best known for his two-volume work, "Democracy in America."

Although some dispute its origin, it is said this quote came from de Tocqueville after visiting America.

I sought for the greatness and genius of America in her commodious harbors and her ample rivers – and it was not there . . . in her fertile fields and boundless forests and it was not there . . . in her rich mines and her vast world commerce – and it was not there . . . in her democratic Congress and her matchless Constitution – and it was not there. Not until I went into the churches of America and heard her pulpits aflame with righteousness did I understand the secret of her genius and power. America is great because she is good, and if America ever ceases to be good, she will cease to be great.

America has been a singularly Christian nation throughout its history.

While other religions were tolerated, Christianity was preferred.

Consider these facts:

• One of Congress's first acts was to print Bibles to get the Gospel to American Indians.

• God or the Divine is mentioned at least once in each of the 50 states constitutions and nearly 200 times overall.

• Thomas Jefferson was a signer of the Declaration of Independence, the Governor of Virginia, Secretary of State, and the United States' third president. He said, *"I am a Christian in the only sense in which He wished anyone to be: sincerely attached to His doctrines in preference to all others."*

• Patrick Henry was a revolutionary general, a ratifier of the Constitution, and the Governor of Virginia. He said, *"Being a Christian... is a character which I prize far above all this world has or can boast."* Also, he said, *"The Bible... is a book worth more than all the other books that were ever printed."*

• John Adams was a signer of the Declaration of Independence, a judge, a signer of the Bill of Rights, and the United States' second president. Consider these quotes.

> *The general principles on which the fathers achieved independence were the general principles of Christianity.*

> *I will avow that I then believed, and now believe, that those general principles of Christianity are as eternal and immutable as the existence and attributes of God.*

> *Without religion, this world would be something not fit to be mentioned in polite company: I mean hell.*

> *The Christian religion is, above all the religions that ever prevailed or existed in ancient or modern times, the religion of wisdom, virtue, equity and humanity.*

> *Suppose a nation in some distant region should take the Bible for their only law book and every member should regulate his conduct by the precepts there exhibited. . . . What a Eutopia – what a Paradise would this region be!*

> *I have examined all religions, and the result is that the Bible is the best book in the world.*

America was not founded on vague "religion" or empty ideas of a god.

America was founded on the principles of Christianity!

> *The highest glory of the American Revolution was this: it connected, in one indissoluble bond, the principles of civil government with the principles of Christianity.*

> *– John Quincy Adams*

The Illinois Supreme Court gave this quote as part of their ruling in a case in 1883.

Our laws and our institutions must necessarily be based upon and embody the teachings of the Redeemer of mankind. It is impossible that it should be otherwise. In this sense and to this extent, our civilizations and our institutions are emphatically Christian.

– Supreme Court

It cannot be emphasized too strongly or too often that this great nation was founded, not by religionists, but by Christians; not on religions, but on the gospel of Jesus Christ!

– Patrick Henry

As the final proof of our Christian heritage, consider the beginning of the Declaration of Independence.

In Congress, July 4, 1776.

The unanimous Declaration of the thirteen united States of America, When in the Course of human events, it becomes necessary for one people to dissolve the political bands which have connected them with another, and to assume among the powers of the earth, the separate and equal station to which the Laws of Nature and of Nature's God entitle them, a decent respect to the opinions of mankind requires that they should declare the causes which impel them to the separation.

We hold these truths to be self-evident, that all men are created equal, that they are endowed by their Creator with certain unalienable Rights, that among these are Life, Liberty and the pursuit of Happiness.--That to secure these rights, Governments are instituted among Men, deriving their just powers from the consent of the governed, --That whenever any Form of Government becomes destructive of these ends, it is the Right of the People to alter or to abolish it, and to institute new Government, laying its foundation on such principles and organizing its powers in such form, as to them shall seem most likely to effect their Safety and Happiness.

God has uniquely blessed America. We have sent more missionaries around the world, heralding the Gospel than any other nation.

However, God's blessing is conditional. If we turn on God as a nation, He will not only withhold His blessings, but pour out His judgment.

4. GOD REJECTED ISRAEL WHEN IT TURNED ON GOD.

God set Israel aside after they rejected the Saviour. Today, He works through Christians and churches.

God has not rejected Israel completely.

Romans 11:1

I say then, Hath God cast away his people? God forbid. For I also am an Israelite, of the seed of Abraham, of the tribe of Benjamin.

God will use Israel again during the Tribulation.

The churches will be gone.

There are 18 mentions of churches in Revelation chapters 1-3. In Revelation 4:1, we see the call to "come up hither."

Revelation 4:1

After this I looked, and, behold, a door was opened in heaven: and the first voice which I heard was as it were of a trumpet talking with me; which said, Come up hither, and I will shew thee things which must be hereafter.

The church is not mentioned again until Revelation 22:16.

Revelation 22:16

I Jesus have sent mine angel to testify unto you these things in the churches. I am the root and the offspring of David, and the bright and morning star.

The churches will be gone so God will use the nation of Israel to complete His work during the Great Tribulation.

Revelation 7:3–10

Saying, Hurt not the earth, neither the sea, nor the trees, till we have sealed the servants of our God in their foreheads. And I heard the number of them which were sealed: and there were sealed an hundred and forty and four thousand of all the tribes of the children of Israel. Of the tribe of Juda were sealed twelve thousand. Of the tribe of Reuben were sealed twelve thousand. Of the tribe of Gad were sealed twelve thousand. Of the tribe of Aser were sealed twelve thousand. Of the tribe of Nepthalim were sealed twelve thousand. Of the tribe of Manasses were sealed twelve thousand. Of the tribe of Simeon were sealed twelve thousand. Of the tribe of

Levi were sealed twelve thousand. Of the tribe of Issachar were sealed twelve thousand. Of the tribe of Zabulon were sealed twelve thousand. Of the tribe of Joseph were sealed twelve thousand. Of the tribe of Benjamin were sealed twelve thousand. After this I beheld, and, lo, a great multitude, which no man could number, of all nations, and kindreds, and people, and tongues, stood before the throne, and before the Lamb, clothed with white robes, and palms in their hands; And cried with a loud voice, saying, Salvation to our God which sitteth upon the throne, and unto the Lamb."

God will call 144,000 Spirit-filled preachers to preach the Gospel during the Tribulation period. The result will be a multitude of Tribulation saints getting saved. Even while the world quakes under the angry hand of God, His loving heart is still seeking and saving the lost who will believe.

5. THE ONLY HOPE FOR AMERICA IS TO TURN BACK TO GOD.

God will use Israel again during the Tribulation.

America has no such promise. God did not make an everlasting covenant with America.

Beware of making your theology revolve around your personal experience. America is not the most important country in the world. Israel is the most important country in God's economy.

New York City is not the most important city in the world. Jerusalem is the most important.

Did you ever wonder why America is not mentioned in the book of Revelation? She is not there. Some think America is mentioned as one of the Babylons, but she would be destroyed even if that were true.

America is living on borrowed time.

America is a Christian nation. It was founded by people seeking religious and social freedom. God has uniquely blessed America over its 244-year history. Yet, we see trouble in our country today. As the godless and idolatrous have gained ground in society, God's blessing has waned.

Our nation's only hope is to turn back to God!

There are two layers of righteousness in a nation.

1. Governmental righteousness.

That is the righteousness of its laws, precepts, and judgments. America is running away from God in this area. Laws that legalize killing babies and promoting sodomy stink in the nostrils of our thrice-holy God.

2. Individual righteousness.

That is the righteousness of a nation's citizens. You cannot control the entire country, but you can manage yourself. Let me encourage you. Your personal righteousness matters! God is looking to the righteous to save America. God would have spared Sodom for ten righteous souls. I don't know how many righteous people it will take to save our country, but you and I can make a start!

2 Chronicles 7:14

If my people, which are called by my name, shall humble themselves, and pray, and seek my face, and turn from their wicked ways; then will I hear from heaven, and will forgive their sin, and will heal their land.

Revival starts with me. It begins with you. We must humble ourselves, pray, seek God's face, and turn from our wicked ways.

Then we must boldly proclaim the Gospel to everyone we know, teaching them to do the same after they are saved.

We change the world by changing OUR world. We save America by saving individual souls.

To what degree are you following the instruction of 2 Chronicles 7:14?

American history is linked to the God of the Bible and Jesus Christ. We have been uniquely blessed as we have followed Him.

There is a growing movement to remove God from our nation and practice. We must not let that happen.

Our only hope is to pray for mercy, turn to God individually, and win others to Christ. Let's get busy!

9

Notes

Notes

CHAPTER 2

God's Plan Of Salvation For A Nation

We Can Still Save America!

Amerrica is a Christian nation. Pilgrims seeking religious and political freedom founded our country. God has uniquely blessed America over its 244-year history.

Yet, we see trouble in our country today. As the godless and idolatrous have gained ground in society, God's blessing has waned.

Our nation's only hope is to turn back to God!

Allow me to remind you that there are two layers of righteousness in a nation.

1. Governmental righteousness.

That is the righteousness of its laws, precepts, and judgments. America is running away from God in this area.

Godless politicians, rogue judges, deep state operatives, and ungodly laws have waged war against the God and Heaven and demand holy justice.

2. Individual righteousness.

That is the righteousness of a nation's citizens. You cannot control the entire country, but you can manage yourself. Let me encourage you. Your personal righteousness matters!

2 Chronicles 7:14 gives us God's plan of salvation for a nation.

If my people, which are called by my name, shall humble themselves, and pray, and seek my face, and turn from their wicked ways; then will I hear from heaven, and will forgive their sin, and will heal their land.

The healing of a nation is dependent upon the conduct of God's people.

Examine the five steps of salvation for a nation in 2 Chronicles 7:14.

1. IF MY PEOPLE, WHICH ARE CALLED BY MY NAME

God is looking to the righteous to save America. Wicked people will always be wicked. The ungodly will live ungodly. God looks to His people to determine the ultimate fate of a nation.

2 Chronicles 16:9

For the eyes of the LORD run to and fro throughout the whole earth, to shew himself strong in the behalf of them whose heart is perfect toward him. Herein thou hast done foolishly: therefore from henceforth thou shalt have wars.

At times, God found people He could use as His instruments of righteousness. Other times, there was no one available for God's purposes. In Ezekiel's day, the LORD couldn't even find someone to pray for Israel.

Ezekiel 22:30

And I sought for a man among them, that should make up the hedge, and stand in the gap before me for the land, that I should not destroy it: but I found none.

God was patient with Israel and Judah until it was almost entirely corrupt. Only a small remnant was faithful, so God purified His people with judgment.

Christians are God's people today.

2 Timothy 2:19

Nevertheless the foundation of God standeth sure, having this seal, The Lord knoweth them that are his. And, Let every one that nameth the name of Christ depart from iniquity.

God looks to His people to determine the ultimate fate of America. Judgment begins at the house of God!

1 Peter 4:17

For the time is come that judgment must begin at the house of God: and if it first begin at us, what shall the end be of them that obey not the gospel of God?

2. HUMBLE THEMSELVES

We must humble ourselves under the corrective hand of God. God hates pride and resists it at every turn. He loves humility and assists the humble.

James 4:6

But he giveth more grace. Wherefore he saith, God resisteth the proud, but giveth grace unto the humble.

Humility mourns over sin. It acknowledges wickedness and seeks restoration.

James 4:9–10

Be afflicted, and mourn, and weep: let your laughter be turned to mourning, and your joy to heaviness. Humble yourselves in the sight of the Lord, and he shall lift you up.

Will we weep for our nation to be saved, or will we weep because it has been destroyed? The choice is ours. Jeremiah lamented the destruction of Jerusalem.

Lamentations 1:12

Is it nothing to you, all ye that pass by? behold, and see If there be any sorrow like unto my sorrow, which is done unto me, Wherewith the LORD hath afflicted me in the day of his fierce anger.

We must weep for America before it is gone. Prayer is the ultimate act of humility.

3. Pray

Meditate upon this amazing fact. God would have spared wicked Sodom for ten righteous souls. To understand the weight of that statement, you must understand how wicked was the city of Sodom. There were five cities situated in the valley of Siddim (Salt Sea): Sodom, Gomorrah, Admah, Zeboiim, and Bela.

Genesis 14:2

That these made war with Bera king of Sodom, and with Birsha king of Gomorrah, Shinab king of Admah, and Shemeber king of Zeboiim, and the king of Bela, which is Zoar.

Sodom is the supreme example of a wicked city in Scripture. The name of Sodom has been forever stained and stigmatized. Have you ever heard of anything pleasant named after Sodom?

Sodom is used as the ultimate illustration of wickedness and an eternal warning of God's judgment.

Deuteronomy 29:23

And that the whole land thereof is brimstone, and salt, and burning, that it is not sown, nor beareth, nor any grass groweth therein, like the overthrow of Sodom, and Gomorrah, Admah, and Zeboim, which the Lord overthrew in his anger, and in his wrath:

Isaiah 1:9–10

Except the LORD of hosts had left unto us a very small remnant, we should have been as Sodom, and we should have been like unto Gomorrah. Hear the word of the LORD, ye rulers of Sodom; give ear unto the law of our God, ye people of Gomorrah.

Jeremiah 23:14

I have seen also in the prophets of Jerusalem an horrible thing: they commit adultery, and walk in lies: they strengthen also the hands of evildoers, that none doth return from his wickedness: they are all of them unto me as Sodom, and the inhabitants thereof as Gomorrah.

Lamentations 4:6

For the punishment of the iniquity of the daughter of my people is greater than the punishment of the sin of Sodom, that was overthrown as in a moment, and no hands stayed on her.

Amos 4:11

I have overthrown some of you, as God overthrew Sodom and Gomorrah, and ye were as a firebrand plucked out of the burning: yet have ye not returned unto me, saith the Lord.

The tragic story of Sodom is used as an illustration in the New Testament also.

Matthew 10:15

Verily I say unto you, It shall be more tolerable for the land of Sodom and Gomorrha in the day of judgment, than for that city.

Mark 6:11

And whosoever shall not receive you, nor hear you, when ye depart thence, shake off the dust under your feet for a testimony against them. Verily I say unto you, It shall be more tolerable for Sodom and Gomorrha in the day of judgment, than for that city.

2 Peter 2:6

And turning the cities of Sodom and Gomorrha into ashes condemned them with an overthrow, making them an ensample unto those that after should live ungodly;

Even the wicked city of Sodom was salvageable by prayers of intercession and righteous living.

Ponder Abraham's Intercession for the righteous in Sodom.

Genesis 18:17–33

And the Lord said, Shall I hide from Abraham that thing which I do; Seeing that Abraham shall surely become a great and mighty nation, and all the nations of the earth shall be blessed in him? For I know him, that he will command his children and his household after him, and they shall keep the way of the Lord, to do justice and judgment; that the Lord may bring upon Abraham that which he hath spoken of him. And the Lord said, Because the cry of Sodom and Gomorrah is great, and because their sin is very grievous; I will go down now, and see whether they have done altogether according to the cry of it, which is come unto me; and if not, I will know. And the men turned their faces from thence, and went toward Sodom: but Abraham stood yet before the Lord.

And Abraham drew near, and said, Wilt thou also destroy the righteous with the wicked? Peradventure there be fifty righteous within the city: wilt thou also destroy and not spare the place for the fifty righteous that are therein? That be far from thee to do after this manner, to slay the righteous with the wicked: and that the righteous should be as the wicked, that be far from thee: Shall not the Judge of all the earth do right? And the Lord said, If I find in Sodom fifty righteous within the city, then I will spare all the place for their sakes. And Abraham answered and said, Behold now, I have taken upon me to speak unto the Lord, which am but dust and ashes: Peradventure there shall lack five of the fifty righteous: wilt thou destroy all the city for lack of five? And he said, If I find there forty and five, I will not destroy it. And he spake unto him yet again, and said, Peradventure there shall be forty found there. And he said, I will not do it for forty's sake. And he said unto him, Oh let not the Lord be angry, and I will speak: Peradventure there shall thirty be found there. And he said, I will not do it, if I find thirty there. And he said, Behold now, I have taken upon me to speak unto the Lord: Peradventure there shall be twenty found there. And he said, I will not destroy it for twenty's sake. And he said, Oh let not the Lord be angry, and I will speak yet but this once: Peradventure ten shall be found there. And he said, I will not destroy it for ten's sake. And the Lord went his way, as soon as he had left communing with Abraham: and Abraham returned unto his place.

We must intercede for our nation! How much time do you spend praying for America?

Nehemiah mourned and prayed after he heard of the destruction of Jerusalem.

Nehemiah 1:4–11

And it came to pass, when I heard these words, that I sat down and wept, and mourned certain days, and fasted, and prayed before the God of heaven, And said, I beseech thee, O LORD God of heaven, the great and terrible God, that keepeth covenant and mercy for them that love him and observe his commandments: Let thine ear now be attentive, and thine eyes open, that thou mayest hear the prayer of thy servant, which I pray before thee now, day and night, for the children of Israel thy servants, and confess the sins of the children of Israel, which we have sinned against thee: both I and my father's house have sinned. We have dealt very corruptly against thee, and have not kept the commandments, nor the statutes, nor the judgments, which thou commandedst thy servant Moses. Remember, I beseech thee, the word that thou commandedst thy servant Moses, saying, If ye transgress, I will scatter you abroad among the nations: But if ye turn unto me, and keep my commandments, and do them; though there were of you cast out unto the uttermost part of the heaven, yet will I gather them from thence, and will bring them unto the place that I have chosen to set my name there. Now these are thy servants and thy people, whom thou hast redeemed by thy great power, and by thy strong hand. O LORD, I beseech thee, let now thine ear be attentive to the prayer of thy servant, and to the prayer of thy servants, who desire to fear thy name: and prosper, I pray thee, thy servant this day, and grant him mercy in the sight of this man. For I was the king's cupbearer.

Consider the elements of Nehemiah's powerful prayer.

1. He wept. :4

2. He mourned. :4

3. He fasted. :4

4. He acknowledged God for Who He is. :5

5. He confessed the sins of the nation & citizens. :6-7

6. He reminded God of His Word. :8-9

7. He reminded God of His People. :10

8. He prayed for wisdom and an open door. :11

4. SEEK MY FACE

Step four of the salvation of a nation is to seek God's face.

King David encouraged the Hebrews to seek God's face after they retrieved the ark of God.

1 Chronicles 16:11

Seek the LORD and his strength, seek his face continually.

During a time of judgment, God pulled back from Israel until they decided to seek His face.

Hosea 5:15

I will go and return to my place, till they acknowledge their offence, and seek my face: in their affliction they will seek me early.

Isaiah 55:6

Seek ye the LORD while he may be found, call ye upon him while he is near:

God wants to be found. He is not hiding. If you seek God with your whole heart, you will find Him.

Jeremiah 29:13

And ye shall seek me, and find me, when ye shall search for me with all your heart.

The word "face" speaks of one's presence. Seeking God's face is to seek His presence.

Psalm 27:8

When thou saidst, Seek ye my face; my heart said unto thee, Thy face, LORD, will I seek.

Psalm 105:4

Seek the LORD, and his strength: seek his face evermore. How beautiful it is to dwell in the glorious presence of God!

Psalm 31:16

Make thy face to shine upon thy servant: save me for thy mercies' sake.

5. TURN FROM THEIR WICKED WAYS

God's people are called to live holy lives.

Deuteronomy 14:2

For thou art an holy people unto the LORD thy God, and the LORD hath chosen thee to be a peculiar people unto himself, above all the nations that are upon the earth.

God expects no less of His people today. We are called to be holy!

1 Peter 1:13–15

Wherefore gird up the loins of your mind, be sober, and hope to the end for the grace that is to be brought unto you at the revelation of Jesus Christ; As obedient children, not fashioning yourselves according to the former lusts in your ignorance: But as he which hath called you is holy, so be ye holy in all manner of conversation;

We are to be a peculiar people wholly given to God.

1 Peter 2:9

But ye are a chosen generation, a royal priesthood, an holy nation, a peculiar people; that ye should shew forth the praises of him who hath called you out of darkness into his marvellous light:

You don't have to turn from your sin to be saved personally. Repentance unto salvation is turning to Christ from idols.

1 Thessalonians 1:9

For they themselves shew of us what manner of entering in we had unto you, and how ye turned to God from idols to serve the living and true God;

We don't get better to get saved. We get saved to get better. God loves us in spite of our sin.

Romans 5:8

But God commendeth his love toward us, in that, while we were yet sinners, Christ died for us.

After salvation, we have the power to quit the sins of the flesh.

Romans 6:6–13

Knowing this, that our old man is crucified with him, that the body of sin might be destroyed, that henceforth we should not serve sin. For he that is dead is freed from sin. Now if we be dead with Christ, we believe that we shall also live with him: Knowing that Christ being raised from the dead dieth no more; death hath no more dominion over him. For in that he died, he died unto sin once: but in that he liveth, he liveth unto God. Likewise reckon ye also yourselves to be dead indeed unto sin, but alive unto God through Jesus Christ our Lord. Let not sin therefore reign in your mortal body, that ye should obey it in the lusts thereof. Neither yield ye your members as instruments of unrighteousness unto sin: but yield yourselves unto God, as those that are alive from the dead, and your members as instruments of righteousness unto God.

You must turn from your sin to be blessed. Repentance unto sanctification is turning from sin to righteousness. God tells sinners to turn from idols. God tells His people to turn from sin.

God's plan of salvation for a nation is to turn from sin.

God saw the repentance of the Ninevites and spared their nation.

Jonah 3:10

And God saw their works, that they turned from their evil way; and God repented of the evil, that he had said that he would do unto them; and he did it not.

Josiah was one of the last kings of Judah. The nation was spiritually destitute after the wicked reign of Manasseh. Josiah ordered the temple to be repaired. In the process, the book of the law was found. After hearing God's law Josiah knew the people were in trouble! He needed to know what God thought.

The spiritual state of Israel was so bad that there was no prophet or priest available. They went to a prophetess to learn God's will.

2 Chronicles 34:19–28

And it came to pass, when the king had heard the words of the law, that he rent his clothes. And the king commanded Hilkiah, and Ahikam the son of Shaphan, and Abdon the son of Micah, and Shaphan the scribe, and Asaiah a servant of the king's, saying, Go, inquire of the LORD for me, and for them that are left in Israel and in Judah, concerning the words of the book that is found: for great is the wrath of the LORD that is poured out upon us, because our fathers have not kept the word of the LORD, to do after all that is written in this book. And Hilkiah, and they that the king had appointed, went to Huldah the prophetess, the wife of Shallum the son of Tikvath, the son of Hasrah, keeper of the wardrobe; (now she dwelt in Jerusalem in the college:) and they spake to her to that effect. And she answered them, Thus saith the LORD God of Israel, Tell ye the man that sent you to me, Thus saith the LORD, Behold, I will bring evil upon this place, and upon the inhabitants thereof, even all the curses that are written in the book which they have read before the king of Judah: Because they have forsaken me, and have burned incense unto other gods, that they might provoke me to anger with all the works of their hands; therefore my wrath shall be poured out upon this place, and shall not be quenched. And as for the king of Judah, who sent you to inquire of the LORD, so shall ye say unto him, Thus saith the LORD God of Israel concerning the words which thou hast heard; Because thine heart was tender, and thou didst humble thyself before God, when thou heardest his words against this place, and against the inhabitants thereof, and humbledst thyself before me, and didst rend thy clothes, and weep before me; I have even heard thee also, saith the LORD. Behold, I will gather thee to thy fathers, and thou shalt be gathered to thy grave in peace, neither shall thine eyes see all the evil that I will bring upon this place, and upon the inhabitants of the same. So they brought the king word again.

Josiah led one of the great revivals in recorded history. God honored the turning from sin and decided to delay the destruction of Judah until Josiah died.

Sin separates us from God. We must turn from our sin to be blessed.

2 Chronicles 7:14

If my people, which are called by my name, shall humble themselves, and pray, and seek my face, and turn from their wicked ways; then will I hear from heaven, and will forgive their sin, and will heal their land.

If we follow the five steps of the salvation of a nation, God will step in and hear from Heaven and heal the land.

I don't know how many righteous people it will take to save our country, but you and I can make a start!

There is nothing wrong with America that an old-fashioned revival could not fix.

Revival starts with me. It begins with you. We must humble ourselves, pray, seek God's face, and turn from our wicked ways.

Then we must boldly proclaim the Gospel to everyone we know, teaching them to do the same after being saved.

We change the world by changing OUR world.

To what degree are you following the instruction of 2 Chronicles 7:14?

Let's get serious about achieving revival, seeking souls, and saving our nation. Start today.

Notes

CHAPTER 3

The Christian & Politics

1 Timothy 2:1–2

I exhort therefore, that, first of all, supplications, prayers, intercessions, and giving of thanks, be made for all men; For kings, and for all that are in authority; that we may lead a quiet and peaceable life in all godliness and honesty.

Politics! Some people love politics, and others hate it. Regardless, all of us are affected by it. Learn the five responsibilities a Christian has in modern politics.

Politics affect every citizen. People elected to government wield real power to affect our every day lives.

Pericles, the Greek Statesmen who lived 495 BC to 425 BC, said, *"Just because you do not take an interest in politics doesn't mean politics won't take an interest in you."*

The laws passed affect you even when you aren't paying attention to the process. Big city politics eventually filter down to the small towns.

Each member of a society should attend to politics to protect liberty.

Let's be honest. Some people are way too involved in politics. You know who you are! You watch 24/7 news, almost 24/7. You can't stop talking about it. You are driving your friends and family crazy!

On the other hand, many people are totally disconnected from politics. They don't care about it. They don't want to hear about it. As a result, they don't take part in the process.

In this Bible study, we will investigate what the Bible has to say about Christians and politics. May God give us understanding to find a balance that is pleasing to Him!

1. PRAY FOR LEADERS.

1 Timothy 2:1–2

I exhort therefore, that, first of all, supplications, prayers, intercessions, and giving of thanks, be made for all men; For kings, and for all that are in authority; that we may lead a quiet and peaceable life in all godliness and honesty.

Prayer changes things. Prayer alters people and circumstances.

God commands us to pray for all men, including our governmental leaders. Why didn't our Lord just stop by saying pray for all men? Why did He specifically mention government officials? He wanted to emphasize our need to pray for them, of course.

Government leaders have a real impact on how we live. They create, interpret, and enforce the laws of the land. If we hope to lead a pleasant life, we must pray for our leaders.

God wants us to lead quiet and peaceable lives. In verse two, the word quiet means tranquil. The word peaceable means undisturbed. A quiet and peaceable life is the best hope for citizens! We must pray that the government will do their job, stay in their lane, and leave the citizens alone to live peacefully.

Christians pray for two more freedoms in a nation. We desire to live in all godliness and honesty.

Ungodly governments overstep the bounds of their creation and involve themselves in the daily lives of citizens.

As the 40th U.S. President, Ronald Reagan said, *"The nine most terrifying words in the English language are: I'm from the government, and I'm here to help."*

Faithless rulers believe that government should take the place of God. They seek to provide money, food, shelter, clothing, and work to every citizen regardless of personal accountability. This "cradle to the grave" approach involves the government in every aspect of life from the womb to the tomb.

How do we stop this intrusion? We must pray!

Pray for current & future government leaders to:

1. Get saved.

2. Know the Scriptures.

3. Follow Christ.

4. Make wise choices.

5. Understand the consequences of their actions.

6. Follow the Constitution.

7. Stay in their lane.

8. Fight temptation.

9. Legislate righteously.

10. Protect our God-given freedoms.

How much time do you spend praying for leaders in our government?

Put them on your prayer list.

Pray for federal, state, and local officials and judges regularly.

2. PARTICIPATE IN POLITICS.

1 Peter 2:17

Honour all men. Love the brotherhood. Fear God. Honour the king.

We should honor all men. We must love our Christian brothers and sisters.

God chose to single out respect for our government leaders in this verse. We should honor the position of governmental authorities, but we should never fear them. God alone is to be feared!

We must honor the position of dishonorable men. But how much better is it to have honorable men as our leaders!

In America, we enjoy the privilege of choosing our own leaders.

Sadly, in many areas of our country today, the masses choose the basest of us as leaders.

William Penn, the founder of the Province of Pennsylvania, said, "Providence has given our people the choice of their rulers, and it is the duty, as well as privilege and interest of a Christian nation to select and prefer Christians for their rulers."

Too often, a slick salesman or a well-funded conman gets voted into office. Americans must have enough common sense to elect honorable, trustworthy, and godly people to government.

To make this happen, Christians must vote in every election. Also, Christians must run for office, so we have good people for whom to vote.

Plato was an Athenian philosopher who lived during the Classical Greek period. He said, *"One of the penalties for refusing to participate in politics is that you end up being governed by your inferiors."*

We are living through that disaster today! I'd rather be governed by an honest farmer with common sense than a life-long politician whose primary goal is retaining power.

Consider these four steps to participating in politics.

Pay Attention

Some people get too caught up with politics. Don't let it control your life or consume you. On the other hand, politics can be discouraging enough to block it out of your life completely.

Find the balance. Stay informed enough to be aware and engaged. Yet, stay sufficiently aloof to protect your spirit. Do what you can and trust God with the rest.

Speak Up

Our country suffers today because good people were silent in the past. God expects Christians to be the moral conscience of a nation.

The silence of the righteous emboldens the speech of the wicked.

Christ's disciples are the salt of the Earth.

Matthew 5:13

Ye are the salt of the earth: but if the salt have lost his savour, wherewith shall it be salted? it is thenceforth good for nothing, but to be cast out, and to be trodden under foot of men.

Salt flavors. Salt preserves. Salt is useful. It is estimated that there are over 14,000 uses for salt. But if salt loses its flavor, it is good for nothing. In Bible days, they would use old salt to harden walkways. Men would literally "walk all over it."

When Christians do not "flavor" our world with God's Truth, we become useless, and the world "walks all over us." We must speak up!

Believers are the light of the world.

Matthew 5:14–16

Ye are the light of the world. A city that is set on an hill cannot be hid. Neither do men light a candle, and put it under a bushel, but on a candlestick; and it giveth light unto all that are in the house. Let your light so shine before men, that they may see your good works, and glorify your Father which is in heaven.

Light makes darkness flee. It reveals the wickedness that hides in the shadows. Wicked people hate the light because it exposes their evil deeds.

Don't let anyone put a bushel over your light. Shine brightly for God! Let people know Who God is and what He says. Let your light shine despite unkind words or open threats!

Don't allow political correctness or cancel culture to stop you from speaking the truth in love.

Pay Taxes

Luke 20:22–25

Is it lawful for us to give tribute unto Caesar, or no? But he perceived their craftiness, and said unto them, Why tempt ye me? Shew me a penny. Whose image and superscription hath it? They answered and said, Caesar's. And he said unto them, Render therefore unto Caesar the things which be Caesar's, and unto God the things which be God's.

Americans are overtaxed and underserved in many areas of the country. Nevertheless, Jesus told us to pay taxes. Some decide to stop paying taxes in civil disobedience. That is not a fight worth the effort for the Christian. We should save our energy and effort for the spiritual battle that wages around us.

Vote In Every Election

Every election is an opportunity to choose your fate.

Alexander Hamilton said, "This process of election affords a moral certainty that the office of President will seldom fall to the lot of any man who is not in an eminent degree endowed with the requisite qualifications.

Regular elections ensure that we can choose moral and qualified leaders.

Thomas Jefferson articulated, *"We do not have government by the majority. We have government by the majority who participate."*

Only those who participate get a voice. If you are a good person who is not voting, you are allowing the other side to win by default.

Abraham Lincoln said, *"The ballot is stronger than the bullet."*

Dwight D. Eisenhower stated, *"The future of this republic is in the hands of the American voter."*

Noah Webster, Adviser to the Founding Fathers of the United States of America and creator of the Webster's Dictionary made the following statement. *"If men of wisdom and knowledge, of moderation and temperance, of patience, fortitude and perseverance, of sobriety and true republican simplicity of manners, of zeal for the honor of the Supreme Being and the welfare of the commonwealth; if men possessed of these other excellent qualities are chosen to fill the seats of government, we may expect that our affairs will rest on a solid and permanent foundation."*

Samuel Adams (1722-1803) said, *"Let each citizen remember at the moment he is offering his vote...that he is executing one of the most solemn trusts in human society for which he is accountable to God and his country."*

Bad things happen when good people don't vote.

One man said, *"Bad officials are elected by good citizens who don't vote."*

Every vote counts. Even when you live in a state where most people vote the opposite of you, don't be discouraged. Vote because it is a right. Vote because it is a privilege. Vote because every vote matters.

Our founders wisely created an Electoral College system to distribute the power of federal elections to every state.

There is a leftist movement to eliminate the Electoral College in favor of the Popular Vote. This would disenfranchise the people in most states in our country by placing the power to decide elections to the largest states and cities. Of course, these places are known for their ungodliness. There is a sinister element at work here.

I live in a state that ALWAYS votes liberally. Yet, I believe it is important to vote.

Why? Voting is a privilege that most people who have ever lived on the planet never experienced. Voting is a right that people have died to protect. Voting is a sacred trust.

Also, every vote is added to the total popular vote.

We must protect the sanctity of our vote. Politicians are always trying to game the system. Do not be deceived.

Here are a few of their tricks:

• Allow illegal immigrants to vote. Of course, most of these will vote for the politicians promising them free things.

• Give U.S. Territories voting rights to add new constituents. There are good reasons that territories are not made equal with states when it comes to voting.

• Change voting districts. As neighborhoods change, politicians change boundaries for their benefit.

• Alter the voting process. Should we trust a fully digital system vulnerable to hacking that is designed by big tech companies with a nefarious political agenda? No. Why do I need to show a picture ID to get on an airplane but not required to show one to vote? Mass mailing tens of millions of ballots is not the same as absentee voting. It creates multiple points of failure, further exposing the voting system to fraud and negligence.

Allow me to reveal another triumph of Satan in American politics.

People are taught to leave their religion outside of the polling booth. WHAT?? How can I separate the most important part of who I am from the sacred right of voting?

On the contrary, we must vote as Christians. People ask, "Are you a Republican or a Democrat?" I answer that I am a Christian.

Learn what the politicians stand for and what they want to do. Next, study the track record of what they actually believe and have accomplished. Separate the advertising from their actions. Compare each of these to God's Word.

Vote for the candidate that most closely aligns with God's Word.

A word of warning: There are no perfect political candidates. Don't stay home because you can't totally agree with a candidate. When you decide not to vote, you are actually voting for the worst candidate.

Cast your vote. Let your voice be heard.

Be involved. Pay attention. Protect your freedoms. Leave the rest up to God.

3. PARTNER WITH YOUR LOCAL CHURCH.

Every Christian should be an active member of a local Church that is true to the Word of God and the Great Commission of Christ.

It is commendable to be a servant of a local church.

Romans 16:1

I commend unto you Phebe our sister, which is a servant of the church which is at Cenchrea:

Each committed Christian should partner with their local church to fulfill the mission of Christ in the community. The church is the hub of the consecrated life.

What does that have to do with politics?

Churches are made up of Christians. Christians should engage in politics. Therefore, churches should participate in politics.

Wicked politicians have worked to keep churches and Christians on the sidelines of American politics. Ungodly people understood that Christians are the moral conscience of our nation. The "do-gooders" needed to be silenced to install their unbiblical agenda in America.

Lyndon B. Johnson was an ungodly politician from Texas who eventually became the United States' 36th president. As a Senator, he introduced a bill to change the tax code to prevent non-profit organizations from endorsing or opposing political candidates. This statute, known as the Johnson Amendment, became law in 1954. Johnson was a skilled politician and an openly ungodly man. His crudeness is legendary. Many believe that Johnson knew he would need to silence the many churches in America to further his political career. He accomplished that with the Johnson act.

A large-scale indoctrination campaign was started that used the Johnson act to scare churches and non-profits to stay out of politics completely. Often, government officials claim more power than the law allows expanding the application of them to further their agenda.

Over the years, I've had well-meaning church members warn me that we will lose our tax-exempt status if I mention politics from the pulpit. (Well done, government. Mission accomplished!) I would lovingly explain what the law really says and then teach them that

Christians must speak up regardless of the consequences. We do not endorse specific candidates or hold political rallies, but we must teach people to see politics through the light of Scripture.

Every pastor and church has a specific mission from God in their community. If your church protests against wickedness, get involved. If your church marches for a cause, join them. If your pastor speaks out, have his back.

Churches must engage in the political process. Partner with your church in this area as you would in areas of ministry.

4. PREACH THE GOSPEL TO EVERY CREATURE.

Mark 16:15

And he said unto them, Go ye into all the world, and preach the gospel to every creature.

Politics have their place, but never mistake them as the answer to the world's ills.

Immorality, cursing, theft, jealousy, covetousness, pride, violence, bigotry, and riots are born in the sinful heart of man.

Luke 6:45

A good man out of the good treasure of his heart bringeth forth that which is good; and an evil man out of the evil treasure of his heart bringeth forth that which is evil: for of the abundance of the heart his mouth speaketh.

You cannot legislate righteousness. Only salvation through the finished work of Jesus Christ can cleanse the heart of man.

Isaiah 1:18

Come now, and let us reason together, saith the Lord: though your sins be as scarlet, they shall be as white as snow; though they be red like crimson, they shall be as wool.

1 John 5:13

These things have I written unto you that believe on the name of the Son of God; that ye may know that ye have eternal life, and that ye may believe on the name of the Son of God.

The Bible clearly says that believing in Jesus Christ is the only way God will forgive sin and allow you to go to Heaven. Religion, baptism, church membership, good works, or financial contributions will not save you. The only thing that will matter at the moment of your death is your personal belief in Jesus Christ.

You can be 100% sure you are going to Heaven starting right now!

If you believe in your heart that Jesus is the Son of God and the Saviour of the world, you should pray the following prayer with all of your heart, trusting Him to forgive you. He will hear your prayer and see your faith. God will keep His promise. You can be sure that you will go to Heaven when you die!

> *Dear Jesus, I confess that I am a sinner, and I do not deserve to go to Heaven. I don't want to go to Hell. I believe that You are the Son of God Who died on the Cross to pay for my sin, that You were buried and rose again. Please forgive all my sins and take me to Heaven when I die. I am trusting you alone as my way to Heaven. Thank you for saving me. Amen.*

Let me know if you put your faith in Christ today!

5. PLAN FOR THE BEST & PREPARE FOR THE WORST & TRUST GOD THROUGH IT ALL.

Matthew 6:33

But seek ye first the kingdom of God, and his righteousness; and all these things shall be added unto you.

Put Christ first. Have hope. Live each day to its fullest. Don't borrow trouble from tomorrow.

Matthew 6:34

Take therefore no thought for the morrow: for the morrow shall take thought for the things of itself. Sufficient unto the day is the evil thereof.

Don't worry about the troubles that may come, but don't be surprised by them either. Prepare for difficulty. Be willing to suffer. Think through your responses before things go wrong. Steel your mind. Prepare to endure hardness.

Above all, trust God. Whoever is running the country does not change your responsibilities before God today.

Politics affect every one of us. If we put our head in the sand, we will be stuck with the results of a process in which we did not participate.

The Biblical formula is clear.

1. Pray for our leaders.

2. Participate in Politics.

3. Partner with your local church.

4. Preach the Gospel to every creature.

5. Plan for the best, prepare for the worst and trust God through it all.

May God give us joy on the journey and grace to remain faithful despite our circumstances!

CHAPTER 4

Is Socialism Biblical?

2 Peter 3:16

As also in all his epistles, speaking in them of these things; in which are some things hard to be understood, which they that are unlearned and unstable wrest, as they do also the other scriptures, unto their own destruction.

There is a lot of talk about socialism today. Many young people see it as a desirable form of government, but do they really understand what socialism is?

Are they aware of its history? Have they considered what the Bible says about socialism?

Some contend that preachers and churches should keep quiet about government. They cite a false idea of the separation of church and state as a reason to keep Christians quiet in the civil realm.

The phrase "Separation of Church and State" is not found in our Constitution, although many think it is.

"The phrase "wall of separation between the church and the state" was originally coined by Thomas Jefferson in a letter to the Danbury Baptists on January 1, 1802. His purpose in this letter was to assuage the fears of the Danbury, Connecticut Baptists, and so he told them that this wall had been erected to protect them. The metaphor was used exclusively to keep the state out of the church's business, not to keep the church out of the state's business." - All About History.com

Christians must be engaged in the affairs of government. We are the salt that preserves righteousness and the light that exposes wickedness.

John Jay, the first Chief Justice of the U.S. Supreme Court, said, *"Providence has given to our people the choice of their rulers, and it is the duty as well as the privilege and interest of our Christian nation, to select and prefer Christians for their rulers."*

There is an organized effort to remove God from public discourse and change history about America's Christian foundation.

Barak Obama (and his administration) was the most hostile American President to the Bible and Christianity in American History.

He said in a speech on June 28, 2006, *"Whatever we once were, we are no longer a Christian nation - at least, not just. We are also a Jewish nation, a Muslim nation, a Buddhist nation, and a Hindu nation, and a nation of nonbelievers."*

America has retained individual freedoms because of its form of government. If this form of government ever changes, so will our freedoms.

For thousands of years, Christians have suffered under despotic governments. We cannot make the same mistakes again.

What is socialism?

Often, it is called communism-lite. It is a forerunner to communism where the government controls everything.

Democratic socialism is a faulty concept that attempts to mix democracy and socialism.

Consider this quote attributed to Alexander Fraser Tytler, Lord Woodhouselee. (1747 – 1813) He was a Scottish advocate, judge, writer, and historian who served as Professor of Universal History, and Greek and Roman Antiquities at the University of Edinburgh.

"A democracy is always temporary in nature; it simply cannot exist as a permanent form of government. A democracy will continue to exist up until the time that voters discover that they can vote themselves generous gifts from the public treasury. From that moment on, the majority always votes for the candidates who promise the most benefits from the public treasury, with the result that every democracy will finally collapse due to loose fiscal policy, which is always followed by a dictatorship."

Also, he is ascribed this illuminating quote.

"The average age of the world's greatest civilizations from the beginning of history has been about 200 years. During those 200 years, these nations always progressed through the following sequence: From bondage to spiritual faith; From spiritual faith to great courage; From courage to liberty; From liberty to abundance; From abundance to selfishness; From selfishness to complacency; From complacency to apathy; From apathy to dependence; From dependence back into bondage."

Can you see this cycle occuring in our country today?

The United States was founded as a republic, not a democracy. Our founding fathers made the important distinction between a democracy and a representative republican form of government. They had studied diligently the various modes of government throughout history. Also, they had a front row seat to the failures of autocracy and Europeon forms of governance.

Democracy becomes a mobocrasy. One man explained that democracy is like three wolves and a pig deciding what to have for dinner. Not such a good idea if you are the pig!

Wisely, the Founding Fathaers created a representative republic based upon our Constitution to protect citizens from the will of wicked people and foolish philosophies such as autocracy, democracy, socialism, and communism.

Don't fall for the utopian promises of the critics of our Christian heritage and Biblical way of life.

Some progressive thinkers will even attempt to say that the Bible promotes socialistic or even communistic principles like government health care for all, a fair wage, minimum income for everyone, godless ideas of "equality," etc.

They strain the scriptures and change definitions trying to make it fit their purposes.

2 Peter 3:16

As also in all his epistles, speaking in them of these things; in which are some things hard to be understood, which they that are unlearned and unstable wrest, as they do also the other scriptures, unto their own destruction.

Socialists envision a utopia. Yet, every time it has been implemented in a country, it fails miserably.

Socialists respond to this criticism by saying that the concepts have never been implemented properly. Implementation is not the problem!

I believe the Bible teaches clearly that socialism is not of God.

While there are many subgroups of socialism with various philosophies, I will address the underlying the concept as a whole.

1. SOCIALISM PROMOTES AN UNBIBLICAL WORLDVIEW

Socialism and communism see man as good and the government as the provider and protector of mankind. These philosophies attempt to replace God with government.

Consider the following flaws of this unbiblical worldview.

A. Socialists say there is no God.

Psalm 14:1

The fool hath said in his heart, There is no God. They are corrupt, they have done abominable works, There is none that doeth good.

The humanistic worldview believes that mankind is evolving into gods.

B. Socialists say government is the provider and protector of man.

Government replaces God in socialism and communism.

We know that God is the giver of all things.

James 1:17

Every good gift and every perfect gift is from above, and cometh down from the Father of lights, with whom is no variableness, neither shadow of turning.

Acts 17:25

Neither is worshipped with men's hands, as though he needed any thing, seeing he giveth to all life, and breath, and all things;

C. Socialists believe government bestows rights.

The founders of America had a different idea. Our founding fathers acknowledged that peoples' rights are from our Creator. Examine the preamble of the Declaration of Independence.

IN CONGRESS, JULY 4, 1776 The unanimous Declaration of the thirteen united States of America

When in the Course of human events it becomes necessary for one people to dissolve the political bands which have connected them with another and to assume among the powers of the earth, the separate and equal station to which the Laws of Nature and of Nature's God entitle them, a decent respect to the opinions of mankind requires that they should declare the causes which impel them to the separation.

We hold these truths to be self-evident, that all men are created equal, that they are endowed by their Creator with certain unalienable Rights, that among these are Life, Liberty and the pursuit of Happiness. — That to secure these rights, Governments are instituted among Men, deriving their just powers from the consent of the governed, — That whenever any Form of Government becomes destructive of these ends, it is the Right of the People to alter or to abolish it, and to institute new Government, laying its foundation on such principles and organizing its powers in such form, as to them shall seem most likely to effect their Safety and Happiness. Prudence, indeed, will dictate that Governments long established should not be changed for light and transient causes; and accordingly all experience hath shewn that mankind are more disposed to suffer, while evils are sufferable than to right themselves by abolishing the forms to which they are accustomed. But when a long train of abuses and usurpations, pursuing invariably the same Object evinces a design to reduce them under absolute Despotism, it is their right, it is their duty, to throw off such Government, and to provide new Guards for their future security.

Government doesn't bestow rights. God gave government to protect those rights given by our Creator.

Even though the Constitution of the United States is a beautiful and profound document, early Americans feared that it allowed the government too much room to take control of people's daily lives and eventually lead to tyranny.

The Bill of Rights introduced 12 amendments to the Constitution on September 25, 1789, to the first Congress to settle the arguments frequently made against it.

This "Bill of Rights" did not give rights to people, but RESTRICTED THE GOVERNMENT.

In the eyes of early Americans, unrestricted government always becomes a problem!

D. Socialists promote materialistic thinking.

Money is the carrot of socialism.

1 Timothy 6:10

For the love of money is the root of all evil: which while some coveted after, they have erred from the faith, and pierced themselves through with many sorrows.

44

Review this quote from an article called "5 Reasons Socialism Is Not Biblical" from the Christian Post.

"According to socialists like Bernie Sanders, the greatest problem in the world is the unequal distribution of wealth.

His website declares: "The issue of wealth and income inequality is the great moral issue of our time, it is the great economic issue of our time, and it is the great political issue of our time."

This betrays a fundamentally materialistic worldview, which is the basis of socialism.

To socialists, all that really exists is the material world. In fact, Karl Marx, the father of socialism/communism, invented the notion of dialectical materialism — the belief that matter contains a creative power within itself. This enabled Marx to eliminate the need for a creator, essentially erasing the existence of anything non-material.

To socialists, suffering is caused by the unequal distribution of stuff — and salvation is achieved by the re-distribution of stuff. There's no acknowledgment of spiritual issues. There's just an assumption that if everyone is given equal stuff, all the problems in society will somehow dissolve."

The goal of socialism is not to make everyone rich, but to make everyone equally poor.

2. SOCIALISM ADVOCATES AN UNBIBILICAL VIEW OF HUMANITY

Socialism relies on the goodness of man to succeed.

However, under socialism a select few get rich as workers make less to support others.

What does the Bible say about man's goodness?

Psalm 53:1–3

The fool hath said in his heart, There is no God. Corrupt are they, and have done abominable iniquity: There is none that doeth good. God looked down from heaven upon the children of men, To see if there were any that did understand, that did seek God. Every one of them is gone back: they are altogether become filthy; There is none that doeth good, no, not one.

Jeremiah 4:22

For my people is foolish, they have not known me; They are sottish

children, and they have none understanding: They are wise to do evil, but to do good they have no knowledge.

Jeremiah 17:9

The heart is deceitful above all things, and desperately wicked: who can know it?

Romans 3:10–12

As it is written, There is none righteous, no, not one: There is none that understandeth, there is none that seeketh after God. They are all gone out of the way, they are together become unprofitable; there is none that doeth good, no, not one.

It is Christ in us that makes us righteous!

Romans 3:21–26

But now the righteousness of God without the law is manifested, being witnessed by the law and the prophets; Even the righteousness of God which is by faith of Jesus Christ unto all and upon all them that believe: for there is no difference: For all have sinned, and come short of the glory of God; Being justified freely by his grace through the redemption that is in Christ Jesus: Whom God hath set forth to be a propitiation through faith in his blood, to declare his righteousness for the remission of sins that are past, through the forbearance of God; To declare, I say, at this time his righteousness: that he might be just, and the justifier of him which believeth in Jesus.

3. SOCIALISM TEACHES AN UNBIBLICAL VIEW OF WORK & REWARD

The Bible teaches that God blesses work and the laborer is worthy of his hire (Luke 10:7).

Our Lord put Adam in the Garden to dress and to keep it. Honest work accomplishes much good in the world and settles the soul of man. He takes pleasure in his accomplishments.

Socialism promises control to the worker, but does the opposite. People who work hard get the same as those who are lazy. This removes the incentive to work and society suffers.

God's plan is that those who work hard enjoy the benefits of hard work.

1 Timothy 5:18

For the scripture saith, Thou shalt not muzzle the ox that treadeth out the corn. And, The labourer is worthy of his reward.

Furthermore, our Lord teaches that if we are faithful in small matters, He will trust us in large ones.

If we are lazy, we will lose money, materials, and opportunities.

Luke 19:23–26

Wherefore then gavest not thou my money into the bank, that at my coming I might have required mine own with usury? And he said unto them that stood by, Take from him the pound, and give it to him that hath ten pounds. (And they said unto him, Lord, he hath ten pounds.) For I say unto you, That unto every one which hath shall be given; and from him that hath not, even that he hath shall be taken away from him.

Socialism is a lie. It promises peace and prosperity, but cannot deliver.

Socialists envision a utopia. Yet, every time it has been implemented in a country it fails miserably.

There's nothing Christian about socialism and Jesus would never support it.

Notes

CHAPTER 5

God & Education

Proverbs 1:7

The fear of the LORD is the beginning of knowledge: but fools despise wisdom and instruction.

Our Creator gave us the ability to learn and ordained teachers to educate us. Unfortunately, in America, the government kicked God out of the school system in 1963. Our country has endured untold suffering since that foolish act. Allow me to make the case that you cannot separate God from genuine education.

Education is vital. It is a necessary element of personal and national growth. The U.S. spends more money on education than any other country in the world. Each child is compelled by law to attend school. But what if the educational system itself has been corrupted?

American education has changed a lot over the years and not for the better. Modern public schools look more like sci-fi indoctrination centers than places of enlightenment. Many of the current problems in America can be traced to the classrooms of the past 30 years.

Abraham Lincoln wisely said, *"The philosophy of the school room in one generation will be the philosophy of government in the next."*

Before we go any further, let's rediscover what education is meant to be.

Dictionary.com gives the following definition.

EDUCATION

1.the act or process of imparting or acquiring general knowledge, developing the powers of reasoning and judgment, and generally of preparing oneself or others intellectually for mature life.

2.the act or process of imparting or acquiring particular knowledge or skills, as for a profession.

3.a degree, level, or kind of schooling: a university education.

4.the result produced by instruction, training, or study: to show one's education.

5.the science or art of teaching; pedagogics.

Webster's 1828 Dictionary offers this definition.

EDUCATION

The bringing up, as of a child; instruction; formation of manners. Education comprehends all that series of instruction and discipline which is intended to enlighten the understanding, correct the temper, and form the manners and habits of youth, and fit them for usefulness in their future stations. To give children a good education in manners, arts and science, is important; to give them a religious education is indispensable; and an immense responsibility rests on parents and guardians who neglect these duties.

Did you notice the difference in these definitions?

Modern education focuses on the transfer of knowledge and years of schooling. Ancient education intended to prepare the person for life. It saw religious education as indispensable. Training in character and manners was considered essential.

Once, education included the training of the entire person for life.

Now, it is a filling of the head with facts. This change is huge.

1. REAL EDUCATION BEGINS WITH GOD.

Proverbs 1:7

The fear of the LORD is the beginning of knowledge: but fools despise wisdom and instruction.

What is THE FEAR OF THE LORD?

The fear of the LORD says, "Since I know Who God is, I am afraid to disobey Him and afraid to disappoint Him."

Secular humanists have effectively removed God from the classroom over the last 60 years.

It is well-documented that the secular coup of the public school system has been disastrous. Public schools began in church buildings. The first school books were filled with Christian concepts and Bible verses. Godless men made a concerted effort to remove God from the classroom and the public arena. In 1963, the Supreme Court established a prohibition on "state-sponsored prayer" in U.S. schools. That decision has been the foundation of the continued effort to remove any positive influence of Jehovah and His Son in schools. The school system has been in decline since they kicked out the Bible and prayer. The American school system is now a mission field.

Some of you are jumping out of your seat right now, citing the Establishment Clause. Sit back down. A nonsensical and unhistorical interpretation of the First Amendment of the Constitution has become the weapon of choice among the enemies of God to remove His influence from our government. Study genuine U.S. history. The first amendment was not added to protect the government from churches, but to protect the churches from the government. Christianity was not only allowed in American government; it was clearly preferred over other religions for much of our history. You don't hear that fact very often, do you?

It is possible to keep learning but never attain the truth. Has there ever been a time with so much education and so little truth?

2 Timothy 3:7

Ever learning, and never able to come to the knowledge of the truth.

This verse has become a reality in modern education.

The Bible warned that people would be willingly ignorant of the truth, especially when it comes to creation and judgment. We witness this willful ignorance often today!

2 Peter 3:5

For this they willingly are ignorant of, that by the word of God the heavens were of old, and the earth standing out of the water and in the water:

Until the late 1900's, nearly every school in America taught creationism. With the rise of the popularity of evolution, some states banned teaching evolution from public schools in the early 1900's. The Scopes Trial of 1925 was a turning point in the discussion. Although more states outlawed the teaching of evolution following the Scopes Trial, the Supreme Court ruled in 1968 that teaching creationism without teaching evolution violated the Establishment Clause of the Constitution. Enemies of God have used that flawed decision to practically outlaw the teaching of creationism on any level in U.S. school systems.

Fake science and faulty theories that remove the existence of God are taught in schools and universities daily.

1 Timothy 6:20

O Timothy, keep that which is committed to thy trust, avoiding profane and vain babblings, and oppositions of science falsely so called:

When asked about the obvious design in the universe, a famous athiest said he's open to the fact that our planet was seeded by an alien race. He is not against design, but he is against design by the God of the Bible.

It takes more faith to believe some of today's "scientific" theories than it does to believe the Bible.

We must know the Word of God. Only the eternal Scriptures can defeat the foolish assertions of godless men. That's why they've worked so hard to keep the Bible out of the classroom.

Titus 1:9

Holding fast the faithful word as he hath been taught, that he may be able by sound doctrine both to exhort and to convince the gainsayers.

2. TRUE EDUCATION CONTINUES WITH GOD.

Proverbs 9:10

The fear of the LORD is the beginning of wisdom: and the knowledge of the holy is understanding.

The goal is wisdom. Wisdom is the application of God's Word to life. It is skillful living. We must teach people how to live!

Facts are useless without wisdom.

Proverbs 4:4–7

He taught me also, and said unto me, Let thine heart retain my words: keep my commandments, and live. Get wisdom, get understanding: forget it not; neither decline from the words of my mouth. Forsake her not, and she shall preserve thee: love her, and she shall keep thee. Wisdom is the principal thing; therefore get wisdom: and with all thy getting get understanding.

We must stop listening to fools who tell us the opposite of what God says. We must prevent godless people from corrupting the mind and hearts of our precious children.

Proverbs 19:27

Cease, my son, to hear the instruction that causeth to err from the words of knowledge.

Knowledge, wisdom, and understanding are necessary to see the world as God does and to live righteously. They work in harmony to give us a full picture of life and how to live.

3. TRUE EDUCATION ENDS WITH GOD.

The Believer's education will end when we see our Lord Jesus Christ in all of His glory.

1 Corinthians 13:12

For now we see through a glass, darkly; but then face to face: now I know in part; but then shall I know even as also I am known.

The Unbeliever's education will end when they see the Righteous Judge at the Great White Throne Judgment. Every knee will bow and confess Jesus Christ as Lord.

Revelation 20:11–15

And I saw a great white throne, and him that sat on it, from whose face the earth and the heaven fled away; and there was found no place for them. And I saw the dead, small and great, stand before God; and the books were opened: and another book was opened, which is the book of life: and the dead were judged out of those things which were written in the books, according to their works. And the sea gave up the dead which were in it; and death and hell delivered up the dead which were in them: and they were judged every man according to their works. And death and hell were cast into the lake of fire. This is the second death. And whosoever was not found written in the book of life was cast into the lake of fire.

There is a direct correlation between the amount of time spent in godless schools and a person's distance from God.

Education is important. Godless education is destroying our nation, hurting our citizens, and speeding souls on their way to Hell.

We must take a stand for genuine education that teaches the truth of God and His Word.

"If we abide by the principles taught in the Bible, our country will go on prospering and to prosper; but if we and our posterity neglect its instructions and authority, no man can tell how sudden a catastrophe may overwhelm us and bury all our glory in profound obscurity." ~ *Noah Webster*

Notes

CHAPTER 6

God Or Government: Which Do We Obey?

Acts 5:29

"Then Peter and the other apostles answered and said, We ought to obey God rather than men."

Government was ordained by God. It has substantial power to protect and punish. But what if it begins to protect the wicked and punish the just? What should Christians do if the Government outlaws obedience to God?

Americans have been blessed to live in a county with freedoms that allow us to worship God according to the Bible and our conscience. But what if that changes? Who would we obey?

In Acts Chapter 4, Peter and John healed a lame man in the name of Christ in a popular public place.

A crowd gathered, and they preached the Gospel. Over five thousand souls were saved!

While the Christians and the new believers rejoiced, the civil authorities moved to stop the work of God. The disciples were detained and ordered by the religious and civil governing body (the Council) to halt all preaching in the name of Christ.

> *Acts 4:16–22*
> *"Saying, What shall we do to these men? for that indeed a notable miracle hath been done by them is manifest to all them that dwell in Jerusalem; and we cannot deny it. But that it spread no further among the people, let us straitly threaten them, that they speak henceforth to no man in this name. And they called them, and commanded them not to speak at all nor teach in the name of Jesus. But Peter and John answered and said unto them, Whether it be right in the sight of God to hearken unto you more than unto God, judge ye. For we cannot but speak the things which we have seen and heard. So when they had further threatened them, they let them go, finding nothing how they might punish them, because of the people: for all men glorified God for that which was done. For the man was above forty years old, on whom this miracle of healing was shewed."*

These government officials wanted to punish the preachers, but the miracle was so public that the happy citizens would have rebelled at such an ungodly action. The Apostles were released with a stern warning to stop preaching in the name of Jesus Christ.

Soul winning, street preaching, and proselytizing was prohibited by law. Jail and torture would be the punishment for obeying God.

What was the Apostles' response? Did they cower in fear? Did they surrender to governmental demands to halt the exercise of their faith?

No! On the contrary, they went back to the rest of the disciples and began to pray for power and boldness to remain faithful during persecution.

> *Acts 4:23–31*
> *"And being let go, they went to their own company, and reported all that the chief priests and elders had said unto them. And when they heard that, they lifted up their voice to God with one*

accord, and said, Lord, thou art God, which hast made heaven, and earth, and the sea, and all that in them is: Who by the mouth of thy servant David hast said, Why did the heathen rage, and the people imagine vain things? The kings of the earth stood up, and the rulers were gathered together against the Lord, and against his Christ. For of a truth against thy holy child Jesus, whom thou hast anointed, both Herod, and Pontius Pilate, with the Gentiles, and the people of Israel, were gathered together, For to do whatsoever thy hand and thy counsel determined before to be done. And now, Lord, behold their threatenings: and grant unto thy servants, that with all boldness they may speak thy word, By stretching forth thine hand to heal; and that signs and wonders may be done by the name of thy holy child Jesus. And when they had prayed, the place was shaken where they were assembled together; and they were all filled with the Holy Ghost, and they spake the word of God with boldness."

These Spirit-filled disciples filled Jerusalem with the doctrine of Christ as they spread the Gospel with power and boldness in spite of government regulation.

God worked mightily as multitudes were saved, and thousands came to Jerusalem from surrounding areas to have their sick healed as the Apostles used the sign gifts to verify the power of the Gospel.

The Council was furious that these religious fanatics did not heed their first warning. In a flex of civil power, the Sadducees arrested the disciples. As a crowd gathered for a public trial, they sent to bring the prisoners. Word came back that they were not in the prison! An angel had set them free the night before.

As these government officials sat there in shock considering their options, a messenger told them that the men who were supposed to be in jail were preaching and teaching Christ publically again!

The Council sent soldiers to arrest these stubborn preachers once again. The soldiers did not stop them in violence, for they feared that the citizens would stone them. These pesky preachers were causing quite a stir in town!

The stuffy, self-absorbed government officials demanded to know why these preachers disobeyed their orders. The answer was quick and straightforward.

WE OUGHT TO OBEY GOD RATHER THAN MEN!

Acts 5:28–29

"Saying, Did not we straitly command you that ye should not teach in this name? and, behold, ye have filled Jerusalem with your doctrine, and intend to bring this man's blood upon us. Then Peter and the other apostles answered and said, We ought to obey God rather than men."

This is the age-old question... *What do Christians do if the government outlaws obedience to God?*

The answer from the Scripture is clear. God trumps government every time.

Yet, how to obey God in spite of government restrictions can be complicated.

Why? Government Is ordained by God. The government has real power given to them by God Himself.

There are three institutions ordained by God:

1. Family

2. Government

3. Church

Each of these have their own jurisdiction and powers. They should not contradict one another, but sometimes they do if one oversteps its bounds.

Government was ordained by God to protect its citizens and punish evildoers.

Romans 13:1–6

"Let every soul be subject unto the higher powers. For there is no power but of God: the powers that be are ordained of God. Whosoever therefore resisteth the power, resisteth the ordinance of God: and they that resist shall receive to themselves damnation. For rulers are not a terror to good works, but to the evil. Wilt thou then not be afraid of the power? do that which is good, and thou shalt have praise of the same: For he is the minister of God to thee for good. But if thou do that which is evil, be afraid; for he beareth not the sword in vain: for he is the minister of God, a

revenger to execute wrath upon him that doeth evil. Wherefore ye must needs be subject, not only for wrath, but also for conscience sake. For for this cause pay ye tribute also: for they are God's ministers, attending continually upon this very thing."

But what if the evildoers begin running the government? This has happened many times in many different places throughout history.

Christians have faced persecution and restriction of religious expression for 2,000 years.

How do these facts affect us in 2020? In America, we have lived in relative peace and prosperity. The coronavirus crisis has been the first time in our lifetime that rights have been infringed in such an overt way.

Originally, Americans agreed to self-quarantine and suspended life because of a common threat. After all, if there is a deadly virus that would kill our loved ones, a wise person would stay home until we found a safe way to move forward.

As more information was gathered, we learned that the virus was not as deadly as once thought. In fact, it seems that many people had already contracted the virus and fought it off without even knowing it.

While many rejoiced over this news, many state governments imposed more strict guidelines instead of relaxing them. What were once "recommendations" started to look like tyrannical edicts.

The question on everyone's mind is, "What do we do if the government continued to demand "compliance" beyond reason?"

It is no secret that some in politics look for every opportunity to change our freedoms in America forcibly. During this episode, local officials have overreached, and police have been confused about enforcing the law.

Consider these events:

- A man sitting on a bench in an empty park drinking a cup of coffee was threatened with an $800 fine if he didn't leave.
- A man was pulled out of a Philedelphia public bus by his feet by 10 police officers for not wearing a mask when the law didn't require it.

- A woman was arrested for driving alone in her car to get out of the house.

- A man was arrested and handcuffed in front of his children for playing catch in public with his daughter.

- Liquor stores and abortion clinics stayed open while the churches are closed.

- Governors in some states banned drive-in church services even though they were within health guidelines.

- Police cars blocked church parking lots on Easter Sunday. Officials threatened to take license numbers and give up to $1000 fines for those who dared attend drive-in services.

- A Church in Greenville, MS had every on duty cop on the church property warning people away from an Easter service. Those who stayed were fined $500. The pastor recorded a police man saying "your rights are suspended."

- When a governer was asked on TV about extreme measures being enforced in light of the Bill of Rights, he replied, "I wasn't thinking about the Bill of Rights."

These things happened in America!

The Bill of Rights was added to the Constitution to quell the people's fears that Government would become a tyranny. Marshall Law has been a concern since its first use in America. Some government employees act like it is in effect when it is not. One police officer was video recorded telling a preacher, "Your constitutional rights have been suspended."

Most Christians complied with government recommendations during the COVID-19 outbreak. It was wise to do so with so many unknowns about the virus. Also, Christians strive to be good citizens. We don't want to cause trouble. Our goal is to save souls not take over governments. We just want to be left alone to serve God in peace.

This crisis has brought to light in our generation a problem that Christians have faced for 2,000 years.

What if the government demands we stop serving God under penalty of law? What if our government forcibly took our freedoms?

What if Christians were told to stop obeying our Saviour under penalty of fines and imprisonment.

It may not happen in your lifetime, but it could. Some expect the Rapture to happen before things get too bad. While that is our blessed hope, it is not guaranteed.

Our Lord warned us of dangerous times before His return. Millions of Christians have lost their freedom and their lives since these words were penned.

2 Timothy 3:1
"This know also, that in the last days perilous times shall come."

The lines have been more clearly drawn during the race riots following the alleged murder of George Floyd by Minneapolis police officers. The same politicians that put their citizens on house arrest don't mind the protests for a cause they agree with. The same people that condemned patriots for peacefully protesting governors' political decisions during such a dangerous pandemic applaud the violent protests that result in injuries, deaths, and property destroyed. The same politicians that believe in open borders, liberal indoctrination, and the removal of God from our society, seem to align themselves with anarchists.

Cities, often run by liberal policians, have been the hardest hit. Citizens in urban areas who have had their 2nd amendment rights restricted found the police could not protect their neighborhoods during crisis.

The world seems to be in chaos as it speeds toward the return of Christ.

What should Christians do? I am not advocating revolt. I am not championing disobedience. I am not recommending lawlessness.

In fact, Christians make the best citizens in free societies. But tyrants fear Christianity because they can never control our hearts and minds even if they confine our bodies. Christians already have a Master. His name is King Jesus!

I am not inciting violence or riot. God's people are called to be peacemakers. However, I am asking a serious question. If the government outlawed the essential practices of our faith, what do we do? What would YOU do?

Here is the crux of the question I am raising. Where is the line between submission and civil disobedience in your life? How much would you take? At what point would you disobey the law to obey God?

Some things are worth fighting for. A few things are worth dying for. What would YOU fight for? Die for?

The Apostle Paul eventually died for His faith. He was ready.

2 Timothy 4:6–7
"For I am now ready to be offered, and the time of my departure is at hand. I have fought a good fight, I have finished my course, I have kept the faith:"

Every committed Christian should know what they are willing to die for. To get you thinking, here are a few areas that we must obey God rather than man.

Confess Christ Publicly

During the Roman inquisition, tribunals were set up by the Catholic church to root out and punish heresy such as confessing Christ alone as Saviour and the rejection of infant baptism. It would look something like this. An offender would be tied to a stake and prepared to be burned alive. As the magistrate or his henchman held a torch, the offender would be given a chance to recant. This means to publically renounce faith in Christ alone and pledge fealty to the Catholic church.

Millions were killed because they would not recant.

Our commitment to profess Christ publically should be more important than life itself.

Preach Christ Boldly

The disciples refused to stop preaching and evangelizing when outlawed. Many times throughout history, Satan has used political intervention in attempts to stop the evangeslistic work of God's people. We must never stop telling the world of our wonderful Saviour.

John Bunyon spent 12 years in the Bedford jail for refusing to take a license to preach. Will we give abandon our holy commission without sacrifice?

Assemble Together Peacefully

God's people assemble in private in hostile countries all over the world. Some at the risk of death. To them, the local church is worth civil disobedience.

In America, some Christians can't be bothered to walk across the street or drive across town in a comfortble automobile. God help us! This lockdown must cause us to reexamine our commitment to attending the House of God. It is something worth keeping at any cost.

Raise Family Biblically

The government has no biblical authority to tell parents how to raise their kids. Leftists and liberals seek to exert their will and instill wicked philosophies into our homes. Some even believe that your kids belong to the public and that parents are a danger to the desired development of children. Do the research. They have already taken over the schools. Public education has more to do with liberal indoctrination that reading, writing, and arithmetic. Do we let them have our living rooms as well?

Make no mistake. The ungodly want your children. We must not give them up without a fight.

Live For Christ Faithfully

The Bible teaches us how to live. Will you allow others to dictate your faithfulness to Christ? We cannot rule the government. We cannot control other people. We are responsible for our own actions before God. Faith obeys God regardless of the consequences.

Which do we obey: God or government?

It is a sobering question. I pray that God will protect our freedoms in America so we can continue to worship our Lord without interference. However, the day will come when you must make a choice.

What are you willing to fight for? What are you willing to die for?

The Bible is full of examples of people who hazarded their lives to obey God.

Consider this summary of the power of faith.

Hebrews 11:32–40

"And what shall I more say? for the time would fail me to tell of Gedeon, and of Barak, and of Samson, and of Jephthae; of David also, and Samuel, and of the prophets: Who through faith subdued kingdoms, wrought righteousness, obtained promises, stopped the mouths of lions, Quenched the violence of fire, escaped the edge of the sword, out of weakness were made strong, waxed valiant in fight, turned to flight the armies of the aliens. Women received their dead raised to life again: and others were tortured, not accepting deliverance; that they might obtain a better resurrection: And others had trial of cruel mockings and scourgings, yea, moreover of bonds and imprisonment: They were stoned, they were sawn asunder, were tempted, were slain with the sword: they wandered about in sheepskins and goatskins; being destitute, afflicted, tormented; (Of whom the world was not worthy:) they wandered in deserts, and in mountains, and in dens and caves of the earth. And these all, having obtained a good report through faith, received not the promise: God having provided some better thing for us, that they without us should not be made perfect."

The examples of the martyrs should embolden and instruct us. May Almighty God empower us to be faithful to Him under any circumstance!

Government was ordained by God. It has substantial power to protect and punish. But what if they begin to protect the wicked and punish the just? What should Christians do if the government outlaws obedience to God?

The Bible answer is plain.

WE OUGHT TO OBEY GOD RATHER THAN MEN.

What should we do today? I am not advocating revolt. I am not championing disobedience. I am not recommending lawlessness. What can we do?

We should speak up against sin, live righteously, win souls, stand for the Truth, and pray!

Pray for wisdom and protection; boldness and power. Pray for our governmental leaders to have wisdom and to let us continue to serve God in freedom and peace. Pray for a space of grace so we can win more people to Jesus Christ.

1 Timothy 2:1–2
"I exhort therefore, that, first of all, supplications, prayers, intercessions, and giving of thanks, be made for all men; For kings, and for all that are in authority; that we may lead a quiet and peaceable life in all godliness and honesty."

CHAPTER 7

How To Deal With A Godless Mob

Acts 14:4–6

But the multitude of the city was divided: and part held with the Jews, and part with the apostles.

The protests and riots in America during 2020 highlight an important question. How do you deal with an angry mob? What does the Bible say?

Interestingly, the Bible has a lot to say about angry mobs and riots. It tells us why they form, how they function, and how to stop them.

Clearly, weak politicians don't know what to do. They have supported them, joined them, and given them what they want, but the mob remains demanding more.

The mayor of Minneapolis, Minnesota, repeatedly gave the mob everything they wanted after the terrible murder of George Floyd. He allowed rioters and looters to destroy part of the city. He apologized for his white privilege, marched with them, and knelt in solidarity. Yet, when he was asked if he supported abolishing the Minneapolis police, he waffled. Then the leader of the mob said, "What did I say? We don't want no mo' police!" She asked again if he would commit to getting rid of the police. When he said no, the MC screamed, "Alright. Get the _____ out of here." He made the long walk to the back of the mob amidst angry boos and jeers.

The mayor of New York City and the City Council defunded the police department of 1 Billion dollars. Yet, the mob said it is not enough. They protested on the day of the decision.

How do you deal with a mob that doesn't fear God, acknowledge His authority, or obey His Word?

Today's mob is fueled by godless people and political revolutionaries bent on changing the fabric of our nation.

Angry mobs can appear anywhere. They can be large or small.

Sometimes the angry mob is at home. The kids can gang up on the parents. One parent and the kids can fight the other parent who wants to please God.

Sometimes there are problems in the church. A few disgruntled people can rally others to their personal cause creating dissension and turmoil in a church.

Although these two scenarios are vastly different, their solutions are the same.

Let's look to the Bible to identify the problems caused by an angry mob and the solutions to this growing problem.

The Problem

It is challenging to deal with any angry mob. People in a mob feed on each other and get more agitated. They make decisions on emotion and stop listening to reason. Things can spiral out of control quickly.

The biggest challenge in dealing with a godless mob is that they don't have foundational beliefs that allow for human decency.

There is no fear of God in a godless mob. They reject the God of Heaven and His Word.

The godless mob rejects the authority of God. Likewise, they deny the authority of man—Anarchists rule in the godless mob.

The godless mob has no historical context because they revise history. They attempt to change the history books and remove statues that remind citizens of our nation's miraculous past.

The godless mob rejects the concept of forgiveness. If you said or did something decades ago that they disagree with, you are irredeemable and must be punished today.

The godless mob allows no room for growth. The mob consists of young adults acting foolishly who seek to punish people who once acted unwisely. They don't permit room for maturity and change over time.

The godless mob has been indoctrinated for many years in liberal and godless philosophy in corrupt schools. These outbursts are the inevitable byproduct of godless teaching.

THE SOLUTION

The Apostle Paul was familiar with angry and godless mobs. Paul was part of an angry mob at the stoning of Stephen in Acts chapters seven and eight. He became a leader of angry mobs rounding up followers of Christ to imprison and kill them.

After his conversion and at the beginning of Paul's preaching ministry, there was a price on his head as the Jews of Damascus laid in wait to kill him. He escaped being let down the wall in a basket.

Acts 9:22–25

But Saul increased the more in strength, and confounded the Jews which dwelt at Damascus, proving that this is very Christ. And after that many days were fulfilled, the Jews took counsel to kill him: But their laying await was known of Saul. And they watched the gates day and night to kill him. Then the disciples took him by night, and let him down by the wall in a basket.

An angry mob expelled Paul and Barnabas from Antioch in Pisidia.

Acts 13:49–51

And the word of the Lord was published throughout all the region. But the Jews stirred up the devout and honourable women, and the chief men of the city, and raised persecution against Paul and Barnabas, and expelled them out of their coasts. But they shook off the dust of their feet against them, and came unto Iconium.

They fled Iconium when an angry mob planned to stone them.

Acts 14:4–6

But the multitude of the city was divided: and part held with the Jews, and part with the apostles. And when there was an assault made both of the Gentiles, and also of the Jews with their rulers, to use them despitefully, and to stone them, They were ware of it, and fled unto Lystra and Derbe, cities of Lycaonia, and unto the region that lieth round about:

When Antioch and Iconium's mob organizers came to Lystra, they moved a mob to stone Paul and left Him for dead.

Acts 14:19

And there came thither certain Jews from Antioch and Iconium, who persuaded the people, and, having stoned Paul, drew him out of the city, supposing he had been dead.

Paul died and visited the third Heaven, but God was not done with him yet.

In Acts 16, Paul and Silas were condemned by an angry mob, arrested and beaten because they healed a demon-possessed girl.

Acts 16:22

And the multitude rose up together against them: and the magistrates rent off their clothes, and commanded to beat them.

Christ saved many souls as Paul preached in Thessalonica, but an angry mob set the entire city in an uproar, and Paul fled to Berea.

Acts 17:4–10

And some of them believed, and consorted with Paul and Silas; and of the devout Greeks a great multitude, and of the chief women not a few.

But the Jews which believed not, moved with envy, took unto them certain lewd fellows of the baser sort, and gathered a company, and set all the city on an uproar, and assaulted the house of Jason, and sought to bring them out to the people. And when they found them not, they drew Jason and certain brethren unto the rulers of the city, crying, These that have turned the world upside down are come hither also; Whom Jason hath received: and these all do contrary to the decrees of Caesar, saying that there is another king, one Jesus. And they troubled the people and the rulers of the city, when they heard these things. And when they had taken security of Jason, and of the other, they let them go. And the brethren immediately sent away Paul and Silas by night unto Berea: who coming thither went into the synagogue of the Jews.

In our text, Demetrius the silversmith started a riot because so many people were getting saved and turning from idolatry. The idolatrous workmen feared losing business.

Acts 19:17–41

And this was known to all the Jews and Greeks also dwelling at Ephesus; and fear fell on them all, and the name of the Lord Jesus was magnified. And many that believed came, and confessed, and shewed their deeds. Many of them also which used curious arts brought their books together, and burned them before all men: and they counted the price of them, and found it fifty thousand pieces of silver. So mightily grew the word of God and prevailed. After these things were ended, Paul purposed in the spirit, when he had passed through Macedonia and Achaia, to go to Jerusalem, saying, After I have been there, I must also see Rome. So he sent into Macedonia two of them that ministered unto him, Timotheus and Erastus; but he himself stayed in Asia for a season. And the same time there arose no small stir about that way. For a certain man named Demetrius, a silversmith, which made silver shrines for Diana, brought no small gain unto the craftsmen; Whom he called together with the workmen of like occupation, and said, Sirs, ye know that by this craft we have our wealth. Moreover ye see and hear, that not alone at Ephesus, but almost throughout all Asia, this Paul hath persuaded and turned away much people, saying that they be no gods, which are made with hands: So that not only this our craft is in danger to be set at nought; but also that the temple of the great goddess Diana should be despised, and her magnificence should be destroyed, whom all Asia and the world worshippeth. And when they heard these sayings, they were full of wrath, and cried out, saying, Great is Diana of the Ephesians. And the whole city was filled with confusion: and having caught Gaius and Aristarchus, men of Macedonia, Paul's companions in travel, they rushed with one accord into the theatre. And when Paul would have entered in unto the people, the disciples suffered him not. And certain of the chief of Asia, which were his friends, sent unto him, desiring him that he would not adventure himself into the theatre. Some therefore cried one thing, and some another: for the assembly was confused; and the more part knew not wherefore they were come together. And they drew Alexander out of the multitude, the Jews putting him forward. And Alexander beckoned with the hand, and would have made his defence unto the people. But when they knew that he was a Jew, all with one voice about the space of two hours cried out, Great is Diana of the Ephesians. And when the townclerk had appeased the people, he said, Ye men of Ephesus, what man is there that knoweth not how that the city of the Ephesians is a worshipper of the great goddess Diana, and of the image which fell down from Jupiter? Seeing then that these things cannot be spoken against, ye ought to be quiet, and to do nothing rashly. For ye have brought hither these men, which are neither robbers of churches, nor yet blasphemers of your goddess. Wherefore if Demetrius, and the craftsmen which are with him, have a matter against any man, the law is open, and there are deputies: let them implead one another. But if ye inquire any thing concerning other matters, it shall be determined in a lawful assembly. For we are in danger to be called in question for this day's uproar, there being no cause whereby we may give an account of this concourse. And when he had thus spoken, he dismissed the assembly."

Notice a few instructive truths in this passage of Scripture.

1. THERE IS ALWAYS SOMEONE WHO STARTS THE RIOT.

There is usually a financial, political, or power goal.

Acts 19:24

For a certain man named Demetrius, a silversmith, which made silver shrines for Diana, brought no small gain unto the craftsmen;

Acts 19:25–27

Whom he called together with the workmen of like occupation, and said, Sirs, ye know that by this craft we have our wealth. Moreover ye see and hear, that not alone at Ephesus, but almost throughout all Asia, this Paul hath persuaded and turned away much people, saying that they be no gods, which are made with hands: So that not only this our craft is in danger to be set at nought; but also that the temple of the great goddess Diana should be despised, and her magnificence should be destroyed, whom all Asia and the world worshippeth.

2. MOBS AND RIOTS CREATE CONFUSION.

Acts 19:29

And the whole city was filled with confusion: and having caught Gaius and Aristarchus, men of Macedonia, Paul's companions in travel, they rushed with one accord into the theatre.

3. OTHERS JOIN THE MOB, NOT EVEN SURE WHY THEY ARE THERE. ANGRY MOBS GIVE THE WICKED COVER TO FURTHER THEIR OWN AGENDA.

Acts 19:32

Some therefore cried one thing, and some another: for the assembly was confused; and the more part knew not wherefore they were come together.

4. INNOCENT PEOPLE GET HURT WHEN AN ANGRY MOB ERUPTS.

Acts 19:29

And the whole city was filled with confusion: and having caught Gaius and Aristarchus, men of Macedonia, Paul's companions in travel, they rushed with one accord into the theatre.

Acts 19:33–34

And they drew Alexander out of the multitude, the Jews putting him forward. And Alexander beckoned with the hand, and would have made his defence unto the people. But when they knew that he was a Jew, all with one voice about the space of two hours cried out, Great is Diana of the Ephesians.

5. PEOPLE GET FOOLISH AND ACT RASHLY IN A MOB. DON'T TAKE PART IN ONE.

Acts 19:36

Seeing then that these things cannot be spoken against, ye ought to be quiet, and to do nothing rashly.

6. OFFICIALS MUST HOLD THE MOB ACCOUNTABLE TO THE LAW.

Acts 19:38–39

Wherefore if Demetrius, and the craftsmen which are with him, have a matter against any man, the law is open, and there are deputies: let them implead one another. But if ye inquire any thing concerning other matters, it shall be determined in a lawful assembly.

7. IMPENDING JUDGMENT IS THE ONLY THING THAT STOPS AN ANGRY MOB. THE ROMANS WERE VICIOUS LAW KEEPERS. PUNISHMENT WOULD HAVE BEEN SEVERE.

Acts 19:40–41

For we are in danger to be called in question for this day's uproar, there being no cause whereby we may give an account of this concourse. And when he had thus spoken, he dismissed the assembly.

8. IF YOU ARE CONFRONTED WITH AN ANGRY MOB, LEAVE IF POSSIBLE. IF YOU CAN'T GO, DEFEND YOURSELF AND YOUR LOVED ONES.

The commandment to "turn the other cheek" speaks of personal offenses. Other commandments teach us to protect those in your care.

9. BECAUSE OF TECHNOLOGY, AN ANGRY MOB CAN ATTACK YOU FROM ANYWHERE FOR ANYTHING.

The same rules apply in every situation.

The Bible describes perfectly the mobs we see in our world today! What can WE do to stop godless mobs from threatening our communities or violently changing our world?

Consider three final thoughts about dealing with an angry mob.

1. DON'T BOW TO THE WISHES OF THE MOB.

Never negotiate with terrorists. Why? It incentivizes more terrorism once you establish that bad behavior gets your attention and gives them what they want.

2. SPEAK THE TRUTH IN LOVE.

The Apostle Paul turned the world upside down by speaking the words of truth and soberness.

Acts 26:25

But he said, I am not mad, most noble Festus; but speak forth the words of truth and soberness. Even though foolish or wicked people reject the truth and call us crazy, we must speak the truth with boldness.

Ephesians 4:15

But speaking the truth in love, may grow up into him in all things, which is the head, even Christ:

Multitudes need to hear the truth. Truth is unfeeling. It hits home hard. Love softens the blow. Most people don't care how much you know until they know how much you care.

Speak the hurtful truth with the unconditional love of God.

Titus 1:9

Holding fast the faithful word as he hath been taught, that he may be able by sound doctrine both to exhort and to convince the gainsayers.

People need to hear the Word of God. Sound doctrine can warn the foolish and convince the opposition.

3. SINGLE OUT INDIVIDUALS & HOLD THEM ACCOUNTABLE.

The mob creates the boldness through ambiguity. If the offenders believe they are anonymous, they will not fear judgment.

Also, the mob provides cover. A small or weak gang member will pick on a much stronger adversary if they know the entire gang is backing them up.

Identifying individuals and bringing them to justice cuts through the ambiguity and removes anonymity. This one simple but powerful action changes the whole equation.

1 Timothy 5:17–20

Let the elders that rule well be counted worthy of double honour, especially they who labour in the word and doctrine. For the scripture saith, Thou shalt not muzzle the ox that treadeth out the corn. And, The labourer is worthy of his reward. Against an elder receive not an accusation, but before two or three witnesses. Them that sin rebuke before all, that others also may fear.

God teaches personal accountability. Each person is held responsible for their actions.

Ezekiel 18:20

*The soul that sinneth, it shall die. The son shall not bear the
iniquity of the father, neither shall the father bear the iniquity of
the son: the righteousness of the righteous shall be upon him,
and the wickedness of the wicked shall be upon him.*

Ezekiel chapter eighteen refutes the Israelites' assertion in Babylonian
captivity that God was unjust to punish the children for the sins
of the fathers. The Almighty explains the principle of personal
responsibility and urges them to turn from their sin.

Angry mobs are scary. Godless mobs are unhinged from the truth.
They can cause a lot of damage to life and property.

Follow these Bible admonitions to stop the damage and protect
your community from mobs large or small.

CHAPTER 8

Has America Changed Her God?

Acts 14:4–6

*But the multitude of the city was
divided: and part held with the Jews,
and part with the apostles.*

America is in turmoil. Riots rage, governors rule with an iron fist, millions of acres burn, towns are underwater, and citizens are divided like never before. What is the problem? What is the solution?

Jeremiah was a prophet during the final days before Judah's destruction and captivity. He warned the nation and its leaders of impending doom. After generations of unrepentant sin, God's judgment was near. The people scoffed at the prophet's message. The leaders ridiculed him and punished him for speaking the truth.

After the destruction of Judah and the carrying away of the best and brightest to Babylon, Jeremiah stayed in destroyed Judah to speak for God. The Book of Lamentations records the unbelievable destruction and the broken heart of the prophet. Jeremiah is known as the weeping prophet.

In our text in Jeremiah chapter 2, our LORD recounts the good memories from Israel's beginning.

Then He asks them two powerful questions.

Jeremiah 2:5

Thus saith the LORD, What iniquity have your fathers found in me, that they are gone far from me, and have walked after vanity, and are become vain?

What did Jehovah do wrong? What sin did they find in Him? None.

They left God because of their sinfulness, not His.

Jeremiah 2:11

Hath a nation changed their gods, which are yet no gods? but my people have changed their glory for that which doth not profit.

Have you changed gods? Do you no longer claim Me as your God? Have you chosen to reject ME in favor of false gods?

Yes. Israel rejected the God of gods to serve the fake gods of surrounding nations.

Changing gods was their great sin!

Judgment was coming. They would be astonished and horribly afraid as they become desolate.

Jeremiah 2:12

Be astonished, O ye heavens, at this, and be horribly afraid, be ye very desolate, saith the LORD.

God had given Israel everything. He called them to be a special people and blessed them above all the nations of the Earth. Yet, Israel committed two evils.

Jeremiah 2:13

For my people have committed two evils; they have forsaken me the fountain of living waters, and hewed them out cisterns, broken cisterns, that can hold no water.

1. They forsook God Almighty Who is the fountain of all good. He is the Creator and Giver of all good things. They rejected Him.

2. They worshipped false gods that were not real. A cistern is a place that holds water. A broken cistern lets the water leak out. God uses the illustration that they rejected the SOURCE of water for a bowl that doesn't even hold water. How foolish!

The consequences of their decision would become a harsh teacher.

Jeremiah 2:19

Thine own wickedness shall correct thee, and thy backslidings shall reprove thee: know therefore and see that it is an evil thing and bitter, that thou hast forsaken the LORD thy God, and that my fear is not in thee, saith the Lord GOD of hosts.

It is an evil and bitter thing to forsake God!

LET'S APPLY THESE THOUGHTS TO OUR NATION.

America is a young country. She is 244 years old in 2020.

While that is old in human years, it is young for a country.

To put our nation's age in perspective, consider these facts.

• Israel was in Egypt for 430 years. That's almost twice as long as America has existed.

• The Israelites have existed for more than 4,000 years. God called Abram to be the head of the new nation around 2100 B.C.

• Egypt has existed for over 4,000 years.

• China has existed for 3,000 years.

America is a baby nation.

Almighty God supernaturally blessed America in her short existence. In less than 200 years, this fledgling nation became the most powerful country on the planet. We have been blessed in every category you can measure.

Our nation's birth was not easy. Our forefathers defeated the most powerful army in the world at the time to earn our freedom.

We have fought many wars to protect our nation and freedom at the cost of millions of lives.

The price to protect our nation has been high.

The deliberations of the Constitutional Convention of 1787 were held in strict secrecy. Consequently, anxious citizens gathered outside Independence Hall when the proceedings ended to learn what had been produced behind closed doors. The answer was provided immediately. A Mrs. Powel of Philadelphia asked Benjamin Franklin, "Well, Doctor, what have we got, a republic or a monarchy?" With no hesitation whatsoever, Franklin responded, "A republic, if you can keep it."

America has battled many foes in physical battles and philosophical warfare.

We have overcome outside forces such as Nazi Germany, Imperialist Japan, Communist Russia, violent Islam, and ambitious China.

The enemy from without could not destroy America.

Today, our nation faces a new enemy - an enemy from within.

America is struggling to find her identity.

Is our nation:

- capitalist or socialist?

- good or evil?

- a republic or a democracy?

And the most vital question of all - Is America still a Christian nation which honors God Almighty?

The answer is all-important.

Psalm 33:12

Blessed is the nation whose God is the LORD; and the people whom he hath chosen for his own inheritance.

America has been blessed because of God Almighty. Our nation has been supernaturally birthed, miraculously protected, and divinely blessed.

But what if America chooses to turn her back on God? What will happen?

The Bible gives us a startling answer.

Psalm 9:17

The wicked shall be turned into hell, and all the nations that forget God.

Other nations could not defeat us, but today, America is being destroyed from within.

Israel made the same mistake!

Hosea 4:6

My people are destroyed for lack of knowledge: because thou hast rejected knowledge, I will also reject thee, that thou shalt be no priest to me: seeing thou hast forgotten the law of thy God, I will also forget thy children.

Hosea 13:9

O Israel, thou hast destroyed thyself; but in me is thine help.

Russian Communist leader, Nikita Khrushchev said, "We will take America without firing a shot. We do not have to invade the U.S. We will destroy you from within."

Islamic leaders have made similar statements. They may be correct. Our nation is convulsing in agony as dissidents attempt to change our nation's fabric by force.

HAS AMERICA CHANGED HER GOD?

It depends upon who you ask.

Ask The Citizens

In a Gallup poll from 2017, 87% of Americans say they believe in God. That number has gone down from 92% in the same survey in 2011.

The real question should be: "How many of those who believe in God are truly saved striving to please Him?"

Ask The Government

Our nation's government has taken a hostile stance against God. Unbelieving politicians and judges have made repeated decisions that defy God and His Word.

• In 1962, the Supreme Court outlawed "school-sponsored" prayer. That decision has been used to keep God out of public education entirely.

• In 1973, the Supreme Court legalized the murder of innocent babies inside their mother's womb.

• In 2015, the Supreme Court made same-sex marriage legal nationwide.

• Representations of The Commandments have been removed from governement buildings across America.

• Crosses have been removed from government land around our country.

"In May 2009, During his first overseas tour since being elected, President Barack Obama took time out to remind Americans and the rest of the world that the United States is not an officially Christian nation.

Speaking at a media event in Turkey April 6, Obama remarked, "I've said before that one of the great strengths of the United States is – although as I mentioned we have a very large Christian population – we do not consider ourselves a Christian nation, or a Jewish nation or a Muslim nation. We consider ourselves a nation of citizens who are bound by ideals and a set of values."

"Not long after that, Obama went on to praise the concept of "a secular country that is respectful of religious freedom, respectful of rule of law, respectful of freedom, upholding these values and being willing to stand up for them in the international stage."

https://www.au.org/church-state/may-2009-church-state/people-events/us-is-not-an-officially-christian-nation-obama-says

Ask The Educational System

Public schools are not supposed to be "religion-free zones," but they have discriminated against Christianity.

Religions from around the world are discussed in Christian schools. Remember when a parent was enraged as her child was taught The Five Pillars of Islam at school? Another parent was horrified when her child was taught to recite Muslim prayers that claimed Allah as the only true god.

Often, ungodly people lead universities and schools.

These godless professors rewrite our nation's history. They incite racism and bigotry with concepts such as the 1619 project.

Students are taught to be biased against God and America. Unfortunately, our schools look more and more like communist indoctrination centers.

History is clear. America was founded by Christians.

Consider these quotes by our Founding Fathers about God and Christ.

John Adams

SIGNER OF THE DECLARATION OF INDEPENDENCE;
JUDGE; DIPLOMAT; ONE OF TWO SIGNERS
OF THE BILL OF RIGHTS; SECOND
PRESIDENT OF THE UNITED STATES

The general principles on which the fathers achieved independence were the general principles of Christianity. I will avow that I then believed, and now believe, that those general principles of Christianity are as eternal and immutable as the existence and attributes of God.

Without religion, this world would be something not fit to be mentioned in polite company: I mean hell.

The Christian religion is, above all the religions that ever prevailed or existed in ancient or modern times, the religion of wisdom, virtue, equity and humanity.

Suppose a nation in some distant region should take the Bible for their only law book and every member should regulate his conduct by the precepts there exhibited. . . . What a Eutopia – what a Paradise would this region be!

I have examined all religions, and the result is that the Bible is the best book in the world.

John Quincy Adams

SIXTH PRESIDENT OF THE UNITED STATES;
DIPLOMAT; SECRETARY OF STATE; U. S. SENATOR;
U. S. REPRESENTATIVE; "OLD MAN ELOQUENT";
"HELL-HOUND OF ABOLITION"

My hopes of a future life are all founded upon the Gospel of Christ and I cannot cavil or quibble away [evade or object to]. . . . the whole tenor of His conduct by which He sometimes positively asserted and at others countenances [permits] His disciples in asserting that He was God.

The hope of a Christian is inseparable from his faith. Whoever believes in the Divine inspiration of the Holy Scriptures must hope that the religion of Jesus shall prevail throughout the earth. Never since the foundation of the world have the prospects of mankind been more encouraging to that hope than they appear to be at the present time. And may the associated distribution of the Bible proceed and prosper till the Lord shall have made "bare His holy arm in the eyes of all the nations, and all the ends of the earth shall see the salvation of our God" [Isaiah 52:10].

In the chain of human events, the birthday of the nation is indissolubly linked with the birthday of the Savior. The Declaration of Independence laid the cornerstone of human government upon the first precepts of Christianity.

Samuel Adams

SIGNER OF THE DECLARATION OF INDEPENDENCE;
FATHER OF THE AMERICAN REVOLUTION;
RATIFIER OF THE U. S. CONSTITUTION;
GOVERNOR OF MASSACHUSETTS

I . . . [rely] upon the merits of Jesus Christ for a pardon of all my sins.

The name of the Lord (says the Scripture) is a strong tower; thither the righteous flee and are safe [Proverbs 18:10]. Let us secure His favor and He will lead us through the journey of this life and at length receive us to a better.

I conceive we cannot better express ourselves than by humbly supplicating the Supreme Ruler of the world . . . that the confusions that are and have been among the nations may be overruled by the promoting and speedily bringing in the holy and happy period when the kingdoms of our Lord and Savior Jesus Christ may be everywhere established, and the people willingly bow to the scepter of Him who is the Prince of Peace.

Samuel Adams called on the State of Massachusetts to pray that . . .

the peaceful and glorious reign of our Divine Redeemer may be known and enjoyed throughout the whole family of mankind. We may with one heart and voice humbly implore His gracious and free pardon through Jesus Christ, supplicating His Divine aid . . . [and] above all to cause the religion of Jesus Christ, in its true spirit, to spread far and wide till the whole earth shall be filled with His glory. With true contrition of heart to confess their sins to God and implore forgiveness through the merits and mediation of Jesus Christ our Savior.

Benjamin Franklin

SIGNER OF THE DECLARATION; DIPLOMAT; PRINTER; SCIENTIST; SIGNER OF THE CONSTITUTION; GOVERNOR OF PENNSYLVANIA

As to Jesus of Nazareth, my opinion of whom you particularly desire, I think the system of morals and His religion as He left them to us, the best the world ever saw or is likely to see.

The body of Benjamin Franklin, printer, like the cover of an old book, its contents torn out and stripped of its lettering and guilding, lies here, food for worms. Yet the work itself shall not be lost; for it will, as he believed, appear once more in a new and more beatiful edition, corrected and amended by the Author. (FRANKLIN'S EULOGY THAT HE WROTE FOR HIMSELF)

John Hancock

SIGNER OF THE DECLARATION OF INDEPENDENCE; PRESIDENT OF CONGRESS; REVOLUTIONARY GENERAL; GOVERNOR OF MASSACHUSETTS

Sensible of the importance of Christian piety and virtue to the order and happiness of a state, I cannot but earnestly commend to you every measure for their support and encouragement.

He called on the entire state to pray "that universal happiness may be established in the world [and] that all may bow to the scepter of our Lord Jesus Christ, and the whole earth be filled with His glory."

Patrick Henry

REVOLUTIONARY GENERAL; LEGISLATOR; "THE VOICE OF LIBERTY"; RATIFIER OF THE U. S. CONSTITUTION; GOVERNOR OF VIRGINIA

Being a Christian... is a character which I prize far above all this world has or can boast.

The Bible... is a book worth more than all the other books that were ever printed.

Righteousness alone can exalt [America] as a nation...Whoever thou art, remember this; and in thy sphere practice virtue thyself, and encourage it in others.

The great pillars of all government and of social life [are] virtue, morality, and religion. This is the armor, my friend, and this alone, that renders us invincible.

This is all the inheritance I can give to my dear family. The religion of Christ can give them one which will make them rich indeed.

Thomas Jefferson

SIGNER OF THE DECLARATION OF INDEPENDENCE;
DIPLOMAT; GOVERNOR OF VIRGINIA; SECRETARY OF
STATE; THIRD PRESIDENT OF THE UNITED STATES

The doctrines of Jesus are simple, and tend all to the happiness of man.

The practice of morality being necessary for the well being of society, He [God] has taken care to impress its precepts so indelibly on our hearts that they shall not be effaced by the subtleties of our brain. We all agree in the obligation of the moral principles of Jesus and nowhere will they be found delivered in greater purity than in His discourses.

I am a Christian in the only sense in which He wished anyone to be: sincerely attached to His doctrines in preference to all others.

I am a real Christian – that is to say, a disciple of the doctrines of Jesus Christ.

George Washington

JUDGE; MEMBER OF THE CONTINENTAL CONGRESS;
COMMANDER-IN-CHIEF OF THE CONTINENTAL ARMY;
PRESIDENT OF THE CONSTITUTIONAL CONVENTION;
FIRST PRESIDENT OF THE UNITED
STATES; "FATHER OF HIS COUNTRY"

You do well to wish to learn our arts and ways of life, and above all, the religion of Jesus Christ. These will make you a greater and happier people than you are.

While we are zealously performing the duties of good citizens and soldiers, we certainly ought not to be inattentive to the higher duties of religion. To the distinguished character of Patriot, it should be our highest glory to add the more distinguished character of Christian.

The blessing and protection of Heaven are at all times necessary but especially so in times of public distress and danger. The General hopes and trusts that every officer and man will endeavor to live and act as becomes a Christian soldier, defending the dearest rights and liberties of his country.

I now make it my earnest prayer that God would... most graciously be pleased to dispose us all to do justice, to love mercy, and to demean ourselves with that charity, humility, and pacific temper of the mind which were the characteristics of the Divine Author of our blessed religion.

Daniel Webster

U. S. SENATOR; SECRETARY OF STATE; "DEFENDER OF THE CONSTITUTION"

[T]he Christian religion – its general principles – must ever be regarded among us as the foundation of civil society.

Whatever makes men good Christians, makes them good citizens.

[T]o the free and universal reading of the Bible... men [are] much indebted for right views of civil liberty.

The Bible is a book... which teaches man his own individual responsibility, his own dignity, and his equality with his fellow man.

Noah Webster

REVOLUTIONARY SOLDIER; JUDGE; LEGISLATOR; EDUCATOR; "SCHOOLMASTER TO AMERICA"

[T]he religion which has introduced civil liberty is the religion of Christ and His apostles... This is genuine Christianity and to this we owe our free constitutions of government.

The moral principles and precepts found in the Scriptures ought to form the basis of all our civil constitutions and laws.

All the... evils which men suffer from vice, crime, ambition, injustice, oppression, slavery and war, proceed from their despising or neglecting the precepts contained in the Bible.

[O]ur citizens should early understand that the genuine source of correct republican principles is the Bible, particularly the New Testament, or the Christian religion.

[T]he Christian religion is the most important and one of the first things in which all children under a free government ought to be instructed. No truth is more evident than that the Christian religion must be the basis of any government intended to secure the rights and privileges of a free people.

The Bible is the chief moral cause of all that is good and the best corrector of all that is evil in human society – the best book for regulating the temporal concerns of men.

[T]he Christian religion... is the basis, or rather the source, of all genuine freedom in government... I am persuaded that no civil government of a republican form can exist and be durable in which the principles of Christianity have not a controlling influence.

For more information about the Christian History of America, visit Wallbuilders.com.

America will be judged harshly for turning away from the God who birthed and sustained her.

America is already being judged. Consider the following facts.

AMERICA IS BURNING. LITERALLY.

In 2019, fires destroyed over seven million acres of our nation.

As I'm writing this in the Fall of 2020, huge swaths of California and Oregon are burning, filling the air for many miles with heavy smoke and turning God's beautiful creation into a hellscape of destruction.

AMERICA IS UNDER WATER BECAUSE OF FLOODS.

Disastrous floods are becoming the norm each year.

"In 2019, there were 14 billion-dollar weather and climate change disasters. Three of them were floods along the Mississippi, Missouri, and Arkansas rivers. Approximately 14 million people were impacted by flooding this year, while 200 million were at risk. At one point in the spring of 2019, the National Oceanic Atmospheric Agency

(NOAA) had warned that two-thirds of the lower 48 states could see flooding."

Race Riots Are Destroying America.

In Minneapolis alone, riots have destroyed 400 businesses and caused damage of over 500 million dollars. Property damage destruction from riots around the country will cost around two billion dollars. The emotional toll on our nation is yet to be known.

Pestilence Is Increasing.

In the last days, there will be deadly illnesses that take many lives.

Forbes.com offered on article on June 6, 2020, called "Coronavirus Pandemic Will Cost U.S. Economy $8 Trillion." Future viruses will ravage the world.

Drought Rages In Areas of America.

According to drought.gov, over 65 million Americans are in drought conditions in 2020. Our coastal community had an outdoor water ban all summer. We lived right by the ocean and didn't have enough water?!

The American Dollar and Economy Are Weakening.

Two of America's primary false gods are money and materialism. God has been judging our financial system. The dollar is on shaky ground. World nations are considering switching to a different monetary unit as the world's currency. The cost of living is up, and wages are down. The rich get richer as the poor get poorer. Billions of dollars can be lost in a moment. Don't trust in the dollar. Trust in God.

WEIRD WEATHER IS ON THE RISE.

Weather patterns have gotten more unpredictable. The world calls it "Climate Change" or "Global Warming." God calls it last days' judgment!

Has America changed her God??

This is the burning question of the hour!

America is already being judged. How much worse does it need to get before people wake up and take notice??

Our nation's only hope is to turn back to God!

You can begin the healing on our nation by following the admonition of 2 Chronicles 7:14 today.

2 Chronicles 7:14

If my people, which are called by my name, shall humble themselves, and pray, and seek my face, and turn from their wicked ways; then will I hear from heaven, and will forgive their sin, and will heal their land.

CHAPTER 9

5 Steps To Heaven

1 John 5:13

"These things have I written unto you that believe on the name of the Son of God; that ye may know that ye have eternal life, and that ye may believe on the name of the Son of God."

Nothing in this life matters if you go to Hell when you die. Are you confident that you will go to Heaven? Do you know what the Bible says about securing your place in eternal bliss?

God made a way for you to know that you are going to Heaven by faith. You may be closer to Heaven than you think! Only five simple steps separate you from eternal joy with God in Heaven.

Follow these steps to settle your eternal destination.

1. THINK ABOUT YOUR SOUL.

"Come now, and let us reason together, saith the LORD: Though your sins be as scarlet, they shall be as white as snow; Though they be red like crimson, they shall be as wool."

Isaiah 1:18

When is the last time you considered the miracle of your existence? Why are you here? Why can you think, reason, and feel far above the animal kingdom? Are you a temporary cosmic accident with no true purpose? Is there nothing beyond the mysterious veil of death?

My friend, you have a lot to think about before you dismiss the afterlife and the eternal destination of your soul!

The Bible teaches that you are a special creation of God. You are here because He wanted you to exist. He has given you an eternal soul that will live forever.

Long after your body expires, you will still be, know, and feel. Your soul includes your personality and the part of you that is reading, understanding these words, and thinking about them right now.

Most people will enter eternity without ever truly thinking about their soul beyond popular quotes, philosophical bullet points, or preconceived ideas.

Take the time to learn what God says in the Bible about salvation before you wager your soul on anything else.

2. REALIZE THE PENALTY FOR SIN IS ETERNAL SEPARATION FROM GOD IN HELL.

The Law of Consequence is evident in your everyday life. When any law is violated there is a penalty. Whether you rob a bank or jump off a bridge, consequences will follow.

Our Creator not only instituted the laws of nature but also has given humanity a set of moral laws. The most basic of them are found in the Ten Commandments. Just as the laws of nature are in effect even if you don't acknowledge them personally, so are God's Laws.

When we break God's Law, it is called a sin. Sin separates us from God and condemns us to pay for our sin. Hell is the fiery eternal abode of those who die in their sin in everlasting torment. God doesn't want you to go to Hell. He made a way for you to go to Heaven when you die.

"... and all liars, shall have their part in the lake which burneth with fire and brimstone: which is the second death."
Revelation 21:8 b

"For the wages of sin is death; but the gift of God is eternal life through Jesus Christ our Lord."
Romans 6:23

3. UNDERSTAND THAT JESUS CHRIST DIED ON THE CROSS TO PAY FOR YOUR SIN.

If you owe money on your electric bill, the company doesn't care who writes the check as long as your account is paid. You owe a debt of sin. The price is death in Hell. Jesus paid your sin debt on the Cross.

When you accept His payment for your sin, your Heavenly account is marked "PAID IN FULL" and your home is reserved in Heaven. When He arose on the third day, Christ proved that He was the Son of God and the Saviour of the world Who has power over death.

"For I delivered unto you first of all that which I also received, how that Christ died for our sins according to the scriptures; And that he was buried, and that he rose again the third day according to the scriptures:"

1 Corinthians 15:3–4

4. SEE YOUR NEED OF JESUS CHRIST AS YOUR PERSONAL SAVIOUR.

You are a sinner who has broken God's Law. The wrath of God abides on you every moment until you accept Christ's payment for your sin.

However, this book in your hand is one more reminder that God is trying to get your attention.

God loves you and wants you to spend eternity with Him in Heaven. Nevertheless, if you reject His love, you will face His fierce wrath.

You have been warned! Don't refuse His repeated attempts to prove His love for you and save you. Do you really want to meet God Almighty face to face after rejecting His Son's sacrifice for you?

"He that believeth on the Son hath everlasting life: and he that believeth not the Son shall not see life; but the wrath of God abideth on him."

John 3:36

5. TRUST CHRIST IN YOUR HEART AS YOUR ONLY HOPE FOR HEAVEN.

The Bible is clear that faith in Jesus Christ is God's plan for your salvation. Good intentions and good works can never overcome your sin debt. When you die, God will not let you into Heaven because you were spiritual, religious, or attended a certain church. You must believe in your heart.

Heart belief is more than a mental assent to the facts about the Lord Jesus. It is a personal confidence that Jesus Christ is exactly Who the Bible claims and that you are trusting Him with the eternal destiny of your soul.

The Five Steps to Heaven are summed up in the word – TRUST.

"That if thou shalt confess with thy mouth the Lord Jesus, and shalt believe in thine heart that God hath raised him from the dead, thou shalt be saved. For with the heart man believeth unto righteousness; and with the mouth confession is made unto salvation. For the scripture saith, Whosoever believeth on him shall not be ashamed. For there is no difference between the Jew and the Greek: for the same Lord over all is rich unto all that call upon him. For whosoever shall call upon the name of the Lord shall be saved." **Romans 10:9–13**

Take the final step right now!

If you believe in your heart that Jesus Christ is the Son of God Who died on the Cross for your sin, you should confess your faith in Him right now and pray asking Him to be your Saviour. He will see your faith, hear your prayer, and reserve your home in Heaven.

Dear JESUS, I confess that I am a sinner and cannot go to Heaven without You. I do not want to go to Hell. I believe that You are the Son of God Who died on the Cross to pay for my sin, that You were buried, and rose again. Please forgive all my sin and take me to Heaven when I die. I am trusting You alone as my way to Heaven. Thank You for saving me. Help me live for you. Amen.

Contact me if you chose to trust Christ as Saviour today. I look forward to rejoicing with you!

CHAPTER 10

Heart Test

2 Chronicles 7:14

If my people, which are called by my name, shall humble themselves, and pray, and seek my face, and turn from their wicked ways; then will I hear from heaven, and will forgive their sin, and will heal their land.

Wide-spread revival begins in the heart of a single Christian. Is your heart ready for revival? God will only save our country when American Christians follow His plan for the salvation of a nation!

Are you following the admonition for revival found in 2 Chronicles 7:14? Search your heart using the following questions as a guide.

Take time to examine your heart. Consider each question. Allow God to guide you. Confess every sin, ask God to forgive you, and request strength for lasting change.

1. HUMBLE THEMSELVES.

How close to God am I right now?

Am I really concerned about revival?

Am I willing to pay the price for revival?

Am I willing to do anything God wants me to do?

Is God FIRST in my plans?

Do I think too highly of myself?

Do I think too lowly of myself?

Do I always need to be the center of attention?

Do I deny myself daily to follow Christ?

Have I asked God for help?

Do my "hurt feelings" keep me from serving God?

Am I willing to forgive any wrong against me or against my family?

Do I look down on others in my heart?

Do I have sinful pride in my heart?

Am I willing to ask forgiveness from those I have wronged?

Am I content with the blessings of God in my life?

Am I fully relying on God today?

Am I filled with the Holy Spirit?

2. PRAY.

Am I committing the sin of prayerlessness?

Do I have a set time to pray each day?

Do I have a specific place to pray each day?

Do I use a prayer list to guide my prayer time?

How much time do I spend in prayer each day?

Do I use a prayer journal?

Do I pray for my enemies?

Do I pray for forgiveness of my sins?

Do I pray for God to forgive the sins of others?

Am I praying for God to forgive and protect my nation?

Am I praying for the leaders of my church, community, and nation?

Do I receive regular answers to prayer?

3. SEEK GOD'S FACE.

Did I seek God's face today?

Have I neglected the Word of God?

Do I desire the blessings of God?

Am I willing to deny myself to please my Lord?

Is it important to me what God thinks?

Do I seek God in my daily decisions?

Do I seek God in my relationships?

Do I seek God's direction for my life?

Do I pursue God as if my life depends on it?

Am I obeying God's Word in my daily life?

Do I show God I love Him by keeping His commandments?

Do I long for God to smile at me because He is pleased with my life?

Do I choose God over sinful pleasure?

4. TURN FROM THEIR WICKED WAYS.

Have I forgiven everyone?

Is all resentment out of my heart?

Am I impatient?

Am I Irritable?

Am I offended easily?

Do I get angry?

Do I hold grudges?

Do I have enmity toward anyone?

Have I been dishonest with God?

Have I broken any promise or pledge made to God or to His church? my family?

Since my emergency or crisis has passed, have I keep the promises I made to God?

Am I envious of anyone?

Am I dishonest with others?

Am I too concerned about things?

Have I paid all my debts to others?

Do I have anything in my possession that does not rightly belong to me?

Do I have any habit which I should forsake?

Is there jealously in my heart?

Do I have sinful pride in my heart?

Have I wronged anyone and failed to make restitution?

Is the reputation of others safe in my hands?

Have I been a talebearer or gossip?

Have I hurt someone, or my church, by needless talk about somone's faults?

Even if it was true, did I glorify God by telling it?

Did I pray for those involved?

Is my heart honest and my mind clean before God?

Are my thoughts pure?

Am I faithful to my wedding vows in deed and in thought?

Do I have any secret sin that I excuse, but should forsake?

Have I forgiven those who talked about me? my family?

Do I have a right attitude toward my fellow church members? my pastor? church leadership?

Do I worry?

Am I anxious about things outside of my control?

Do I complain?

Am I guilty of the sin of unbelief?

Have I honestly tried to be a good witness for Christ?

It is a wonderful thing to be right with God. What peace and joy comes through full submission to Christ!

May God give us revival in our hearts that will spread throughout the land!

About The Author

Paul E. Chapman loves helping committed Christians reach their potential, fulfill God's will, and change their world.

He has served as the pastor of Curtis Corner Baptist Church since May of 2004. He and his wife, Sarah, have three precious children and live in a coastal community in the beautiful state of Rhode Island.

They have a passion to reach the lost for Christ, to teach believers to live by faith, and to train God's people for the work of the ministry.

Sarah has had a unique blend of aggressive autoimmune diseases since 2008 that leave her bedbound 95% of the time in constant debilitating pain. Their family's testimony of faithfulness to God has been an encouragement to many.

Paul writes weekly on his website and uses his unique blend of talents for God through various ministries and enterprises.

Learn more at www.PaulEChapman.com.

thepaulechapman

Also Available From This Author

THIS MINI-BOOK WILL HELP YOU
SEE MORE PEOPLE SAVED.

The "Ye Must Be Born Again" mini-book was written to help you fulfill your mission of spreading the Gospel. Whether you are a Christian concerned for your friends and family, or a pastor looking for a new tool to help your church win souls, this mini-book is for you! It includes a crystal-clear presentation of the Gospel, a moving plea to accept Christ, powerful reasons for assurance of salvation, and first-steps for new converts.

ORDER YOURS TODAY AT ADDTOYOURFAITH.COM.

Also Available From This Author

JUST SAY NO!
FORTY DAYS TO VICTORY
OVER TEMPTATION

This is a devotional book designed to give a daily Minimum Effective Dose (MED) of Bible truth on the subject of temptation. Every chapter is a call to say NO to sin. Trust God for the victory. With His help, you can create lasting, positive change in your life. Once you have the victory, you can help others find it as well.

ORDER YOURS TODAY AT ADDTOYOURFAITH.COM.

Also Available From This Author

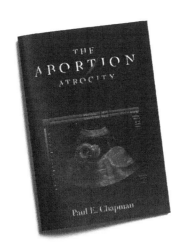

THIS SHOCKING MINI-BOOK SETTLES THE
CONTENTOUS ISSUE OF ABORTION.

The Abortion Atrocity exposes the truth behind the evil practice of
abortion and gives you ten statements founded on the Word of God
that settle the abortion issue.

At a time when our nation is at a crossroads, we need to be personally
informed and do what we can to explain God's view on abortion to
others.

GET BULK DISCOUNTS AT ADDTOYOURFAITH.COM.

Notes

Notes

Made in the USA
Middletown, DE
10 May 2023

30280689R00066